WELCOME TO THE DESERT
OF THE REAL!

Appearing on the first anniversary of the attacks on the World Trade Center and the Pentagon, these three books from Verso present analyses of the United States, the media, and the events surrounding September 11 by Europe's most stimulating and provocative philosophers. Probing beneath the level of TV commentary, political and cultural orthodoxies, and 'rent-a-quote' punditry, Jean Baudrillard, Paul Virilio and Slavoj Žižek offer three highly original and readable accounts that serve as both fascinating introductions to the direction of their respective projects and insightful critiques of the unfolding events. This series seeks to comprehend the philosophical meaning of September 11 and will leave untouched none of the prevailing views currently propagated.

THE SPIRIT OF TERRORISM
Jean Baudrillard

GROUND ZERO
Paul Virilio

WELCOME TO THE DESERT
OF THE REAL!
Slavoj Žižek

WELCOME TO THE DESERT OF THE REAL!

FIVE ESSAYS ON SEPTEMBER 11 AND RELATED DATES

◆

SLAVOJ ŽIŽEK

VERSO

London • New York

To Pamela Pascoe and Eric Santner,
without any doubt!

First published by Verso 2002
© Slavoj Žižek
All rights reserved

The moral rights of the author have been asserted

1 3 5 7 9 10 8 6 4 2

Verso
UK: 6 Meard Street, London W1F 0EG
USA: 180 Varick Street, New York, NY 10014–4606
www.versobooks.com

Verso is the imprint of New Left Books

ISBN 1–85984–421–9

British Library Cataloguing in Publication Data
A catalogue record for this book is available
from the British Library

Library of Congress Cataloging-in-Publication Data
A catalog record for this book is available
from the Library of Congress

Typeset in Perpetua by M Rules
Printed and bound in the UK by
Biddles Ltd, Guildford and King's Lynn
www.biddles.co.uk

CONTENTS

INTRODUCTION:
THE MISSING INK

In an old joke from the defunct German Democratic Republic, a German worker gets a job in Siberia; aware of how all mail will be read by the censors, he tells his friends: 'Let's establish a code: if a letter you get from me is written in ordinary blue ink, it's true; if it's written in red ink, it's false.' After a month, his friends get the first letter, written in blue ink: 'Everything is wonderful here: the shops are full, food is abundant, apartments are large and properly heated, cinemas show films from the West, there are many beautiful girls ready for an affair – the only thing you can't get is *red ink*.' The structure here is more refined than it might appear: although the worker is unable to signal that what he is saying is a lie in the prearranged way, he none the less succeeds in getting his message across – how? *By inscribing the very reference to the code into the encoded message, as one of its elements.* Of course, this is the standard problem of self-reference: since the letter is written in blue, is its entire content therefore not true? The answer is that the very fact that the lack of red ink is mentioned signals that it *should* have been written in red ink. The nice point is that this mention of the lack of red ink produces the effect of truth *independently of its own literal truth*:

even if red ink really *was* available, the lie that it is unavailable is
the only way to get the true message across in this specific condition of censorship.

Is this not the matrix of an efficient critique of ideology – not
only in 'totalitarian' conditions of censorship but, perhaps even
more, in the more refined conditions of liberal censorship? One
starts by agreeing that one has all the freedoms one wants – then
one merely adds that the only thing missing is the 'red ink': we
'feel free' because we lack the very language to articulate our
unfreedom. What this lack of red ink means is that, today, all the
main terms we use to designate the present conflict – 'war on
terrorism', 'democracy and freedom', 'human rights', and so
on – are false terms, mystifying our perception of the situation
instead of allowing us to think it. In this precise sense, our 'freedoms' themselves serve to mask and sustain our deeper
unfreedom. A hundred years ago, in his emphasis on the acceptance of some fixed dogma as the condition of (demanding)
actual freedom, Gilbert Keith Chesterton perspicuously
detected the antidemocratic potential of the very principle of
freedom of thought:

> We may say broadly that free thought is the best of all safe-
> guards against freedom. Managed in a modern style, the
> emancipation of the slave's mind is the best way of prevent-
> ing the emancipation of the slave. Teach him to worry about
> whether he wants to be free, and he will not free himself.[1]

Is this not emphatically true of our 'postmodern' time, with its
freedom to deconstruct, doubt, distantiate oneself? We should
not forget that Chesterton makes exactly the same claim as Kant

1   Gilbert Keith Chesterton, *Orthodoxy*, San Francisco: Ignatius Press
1995, p. 114.

in his 'What is Enlightenment?': 'Think as much as you like, and as freely as you like, just obey!' The only difference is that Chesterton is more specific, and spells out the implicit paradox beneath the Kantian reasoning: not only does freedom of thought not undermine actual social servitude, it positively sustains it. The old motto 'Don't think, obey!' to which Kant reacts is counterproductive: it effectively breeds rebellion; the only way to secure social servitude is through freedom of thought. Chesterton is also logical enough to assert the obverse of Kant's motto: the struggle for freedom needs a reference to some unquestionable dogma.

In a classic line from a Hollywood screwball comedy, the girl asks her boyfriend: 'Do you want to marry me?' 'No!' 'Stop dodging the issue! Give me a straight answer!' In a way, the underlying logic is correct: the only acceptable straight answer for the girl is 'Yes!', so anything else, including a straight 'No!', counts as evasion. This underlying logic, of course, is again that of the forced choice: you're free to decide, on condition that you make the right choice. Would not a priest rely on the same paradox in a dispute with a sceptical layman? 'Do you believe in God?' 'No.' 'Stop dodging the issue! Give me a straight answer!' Again, in the opinion of the priest, the only straight answer is to assert one's belief in God: far from standing for a clear symmetrical stance, the atheist's denial of belief is an attempt to dodge the issue of the divine encounter. And is it not the same today with the choice 'democracy or fundamentalism'? Is it not that, within the terms of this choice, it is simply not possible to choose 'fundamentalism'? What is problematic in the way the ruling ideology imposes this choice on us is not 'fundamentalism' but, rather, *democracy itself*: as if the only alternative to 'fundamentalism' is the political system of liberal parliamentary democracy.

1

PASSIONS OF THE REAL, PASSIONS OF SEMBLANCE

When Brecht, on the way from his home to his theatre in July 1953, passed the column of Soviet tanks rolling towards the *Stalinallee* to crush the workers' rebellion, he waved at them and wrote in his diary later that day that, at that moment, he (never a party member) was tempted for the first time in his life to join the Communist Party. It was not that Brecht tolerated the cruelty of the struggle in the hope that it would bring a prosperous future: the harshness of the violence as such was perceived and endorsed as a sign of authenticity. . . . Is this not an exemplary case of what Alain Badiou has identified as the key feature of the twentieth century: the 'passion for the Real [*la passion du réel*]'?[2] In contrast to the nineteenth century of utopian or 'scientific' projects and ideals, plans for the future, the twentieth century aimed at delivering the thing itself – at directly realizing the longed-for New Order. The ultimate and defining moment of the twentieth century was the direct experience of the Real as opposed to everyday social reality – the Real in its extreme

2 See Alain Badiou, *Le siécle*, forthcoming from Éditions du Seuil, Paris.

violence as the price to be paid for peeling off the deceptive
layers of reality.

In the trenches of World War I, Ernst Jünger was already celebrating face-to-face combat as the authentic intersubjective
encounter: authenticity resides in the act of violent transgression, from the Lacanian Real – the Thing Antigone confronts
when she violates the order of the City – to the Bataillean
excess. In the domain of sexuality itself, the icon of this 'passion
for the real' is Oshima's *Empire of the Senses*, a Japanese cult
movie from the 1970s in which the couple's love relationship is
radicalized into mutual torture until death. Is not the ultimate
figure of the passion for the Real the option we get on hardcore
websites to observe the inside of a vagina from the vantage point
of a tiny camera at the top of the penetrating dildo? At this
extreme point, a shift occurs: when we get too close to the
desired object, erotic fascination turns into disgust at the Real of
the bare flesh.[3]

Another version of the 'passion for the Real' as opposed to
the 'servicing of goods' in social reality is clearly discernible in
the Cuban revolution. Making virtue out of necessity, today's
Cuba heroically continues to defy the capitalist logic of waste
and planned obsolescence: many of the products used there are,
in the West, treated as waste – not only the proverbial 1950s
American cars which magically still function, but even dozens of
Canadian yellow school buses (with old painted inscriptions in
French or English, still completely legible), probably given as a

3 And, to add a personal note: when, in the early 1990s, I was more
   involved in Slovene politics, I experienced my own brush with the
   passion for the Real: when I was considered for a government post,
   the only one which interested me was that of the Minister of the
   Interior or head of the secret service – the notion of serving as
   Minister of culture, education, or science seemed to me utterly
   ridiculous, not even worth serious consideration.

present to Cuba and used there for public transport.[4] Thus we have the paradox that, in the frantic era of global capitalism, the main result of the revolution is to bring social dynamics to a standstill – the price to be paid for exclusion from the global capitalist network. Here we encounter a strange symmetry between Cuba and Western 'postindustrial' societies: in both cases, the frantic mobilization conceals a more fundamental immobility. In Cuba, revolutionary mobilization conceals social stasis; in the developed West, frantic social activity conceals the basic sameness of global capitalism, the absence of an Event. . . .

Walter Benjamin defined the Messianic moment as that of *Dialektik im Stillstand*, dialectics at a standstill: in the expectation of a Messianic Event, life comes to a standstill. Do we not encounter in Cuba a strange realization of this, a kind of negative Messianic time: the social standstill in which 'the end of time is near' and everybody is waiting for the Miracle of what will happen when Castro dies, and socialism collapses? No wonder that, besides political news and reports, the main item on Cuban TV is English-language courses – an incredible number of them, five to six hours every day. Paradoxically, the very return to anti-Messianic capitalist normality is experienced as the object

---

4 This externality to capitalism is also discernible in the way Cuba continues to rely on the good old Socialist stance of symbolic accountancy: in order to count properly, every event has to be inscribed into the big Other. There was a note on a display panel in a Havana hotel in 2001: 'Dear guests, in order to fulfil the program of fumigation for this hotel, the hotel will be fumigated on February 9 from 3 p.m. till 9 p.m.' Why this redoubling? Why not simply inform the guests that the hotel will be fumigated? Why should fumigation be covered by a 'program of fumigation'? (And, incidentally, I am tempted to ask if this is also how one proposes a sexual encounter in these conditions: not the usual process of seduction, but 'My dear, in order to fulfil our sexual programme, why don't we . . .' .)

of Messianic expectation – something for which the country simply waits, in a state of frozen animation.

In Cuba, renunciations themselves are experienced/ imposed as proof of the authenticity of the revolutionary Event – what, in psychoanalysis, is called the logic of castration. The entire Cuban politico-ideological identity rests on the fidelity to castration (no wonder the Leader is called Fidel Castro!): the counterpart of the Event is the growing inertia of social being/life: a country frozen in time, with old buildings in a state of decay. It is not that the revolutionary Event was 'betrayed' by the Thermidorian establishment of a new order; the very insistence on the Event led to the immobilization at the level of positive social being. The decaying houses *are* the proof of fidelity to the Event. No wonder revolutionary iconography in today's Cuba is full of Christian references – apostles of the Revolution, the elevation of Che into a Christlike figure, the Eternal One ('lo Eterno' – the title of a song Carlos Puebla sings about him): when Eternity intervenes in time, time comes to a standstill. No wonder that the basic impression of Havana in 2001 was that the original inhabitants had escaped, and *squatters had taken it over* – out of place in these magnificent old buildings, occupying them temporarily, subdividing large spaces with wooden panels, and so on. Here, the image of Cuba we get from someone like Pedro Juan Gutiérrez (his 'dirty Havana trilogy') is revealing: the Cuban 'being' as opposed to the revolutionary Event – the daily struggle for survival, the escape into violent promiscuous sex, seizing the day without future-oriented projects. This obscene inertia is the 'truth' of the revolutionary Sublime.[5]

---

5   The specificity of the Cuban revolution is best expressed by the duality of Fidel and Che Guevara: Fidel, the actual Leader, supreme authority of the State, versus Che, the eternal revolutionary rebel who could not resign himself to just running a state. Is this not

And is not so-called fundamentalist terror also an expression of the passion for the Real? Back in the early 1970s, after the collapse of the New Left student protest movement in Germany, one of its outgrowths was the Red Army Faction terrorism (the Baader–Meinhof 'gang', and so on); its underlying premise was that the failure of the student movement had demonstrated that the masses were so deeply immersed in their apolitical consumerist stance that it was not possible to awaken them through standard political education and consciousness-raising – a more violent intervention was needed to shake them out of their ideological numbness, their hypnotic consumerist state, and only direct violent interventions like bombing supermarkets would do the job. And does the same not hold, on a different level, for today's fundamentalist terror? Is not its goal also to awaken us, Western citizens, from our numbness, from immersion in our everyday ideological universe?

These last two examples indicate the fundamental paradox of the 'passion for the Real': it culminates in its apparent opposite, in a *theatrical spectacle* – from the Stalinist show trials to spectacular terrorist acts.[6] If, then, the passion for the Real ends up

something like a Soviet Union in which Trotsky would not have been rejected as the arch-traitor? Imagine that, in the mid 1920s, Trotsky had emigrated and renounced Soviet citizenship in order to incite permanent revolution around the world, and then died soon afterwards – after his death, Stalin would have elevated him into a cult. . . . Of course, such a fidelity to the Cause ('Socialismo o muerte!'), in so far as this Cause is embodied in the Leader, can easily degenerate into the Leader's readiness to sacrifice (not himself for the country, but) the country itself for himself, for his Cause. (Similarly, the proof of true fidelity to a Leader is not that one is ready to take a bullet *for* him; over and above this, one must be ready to take a bullet *from* him – accept being dropped or even sacrificed by him if this serves his higher purposes.)

6 On a more general level, we should note how Stalinism – with its brutal 'passion for the Real', its readiness to sacrifice millions of lives for its goal, to treat people as dispensable – was at the same

in the pure semblance of the spectacular *effect of the Real*, then, in an exact inversion, the 'postmodern' passion for the semblance ends up in a violent return to the passion for the Real. Take the phenomenon of 'cutters' (people, mostly women, who experience an irresistible urge to cut themselves with razors or otherwise hurt themselves); this is strictly parallel to the virtualization of our environment: it represents a desperate strategy to return to the Real of the body. As such, cutting must be contrasted with normal tattooed inscriptions on the body, which guarantee the subject's inclusion in the (virtual) symbolic order – the problem with cutters, is the opposite one, namely, the assertion of reality itself. Far from being suicidal, far from indicating a desire for self-annihilation, cutting is a radical attempt to (re)gain a hold on reality, or (another aspect of the same phenomenon) to ground the ego firmly in bodily reality, against the unbearable anxiety of perceiving oneself as nonexistent. Cutters usually say that once they see the warm red blood flowing out of the self-inflicted wound, they feel alive again, firmly rooted in reality.[7] So although, of course, cutting is a pathological phenomenon, it is none the less a pathological attempt at regaining some kind of normality, at avoiding a total psychotic breakdown.

On today's market, we find a whole series of products deprived of their malignant properties: coffee without caffeine, cream without fat, beer without alcohol. . . . And the list goes on: what about virtual sex as sex without sex, the Colin Powell

time the regime most sensitive about *maintaining proper appearances*: it reacted with total panic whenever there was a threat that these appearances would be disturbed (say, that some accident which clearly revealed the failure of the regime would be reported in the media: in the Soviet media there were no black chronicles, no reports on crime and prostitution, let alone workers' or public protests).

7 See Marilee Strong, *The Bright Red Scream*, London: Virago 2000.

doctrine of warfare with no casualties (on our side, of course) as warfare without warfare, the contemporary redefinition of politics as the art of expert administration, that is, as politics without politics, up to today's tolerant liberal multiculturalism as an experience of the Other deprived of its Otherness (the idealized Other who dances fascinating dances and has an ecologically sound holistic approach to reality, while practices like wife beating remain out of sight . . .)? Virtual Reality simply generalizes this procedure of offering a product deprived of its substance: it provides reality itself deprived of its substance, of the hard resistant kernel of the Real – just as decaffeinated coffee smells and tastes like real coffee without being real coffee, Virtual Reality is experienced as reality without being so. What happens at the end of this process of virtualization, however, is that we begin to experience 'real reality' itself as a virtual entity. For the great majority of the public, the WTC explosions were events on the TV screen, and when we watched the oft-repeated shot of frightened people running towards the camera ahead of the giant cloud of dust from the collapsing tower, was not the framing of the shot itself reminiscent of spectacular shots in catastrophe movies, a special effect which outdid all others, since – as Jeremy Bentham knew – reality is the best appearance of itself?

And was not the attack on the World Trade Center with regard to Hollywood catastrophe movies like snuff pornography versus ordinary sado-masochistic porno movies? This is the element of truth in Karl-Heinz Stockhausen's provocative statement that the planes hitting the WTC towers was the ultimate work of art: we can perceive the collapse of the WTC towers as the climactic conclusion of twentieth-century art's 'passion for the Real' – the 'terrorists' themselves did not do it primarily to provoke real material damage, but *for the spectacular effect of it*. When, days after September 11 2001, our gaze was transfixed by the images of the plane hitting one of the

WTC towers, we were all forced to experience what the 'compulsion to repeat' and *jouissance* beyond the pleasure principle are: we wanted to see it again and again; the same shots were repeated *ad nauseam*, and the uncanny satisfaction we got from it was *jouissance* at its purest. It was when we watched the two WTC towers collapsing on the TV screen, that it became possible to experience the falsity of 'reality TV shows': even if these shows are 'for real', people still act in them – they simply play themselves. The standard disclaimer in a novel ('Characters in this text are fictional, any resemblance to real-life characters is purely accidental') also holds for participants in reality soaps: what we see there are fictional characters, even if they play themselves for real.

The authentic twentieth-century passion for penetrating the Real Thing (ultimately, the destructive Void) through the cobweb of semblances which constitutes our reality thus culminates in the thrill of the Real as the ultimate 'effect', sought after from digitalized special effects, through reality TV and amateur pornography, up to snuff movies. Snuff movies which deliver the 'real thing' are perhaps the ultimate truth of Virtual Reality. There is an intimate connection between the virtualization of reality and the emergence of an infinite and infinitized bodily pain, much stronger than the usual one: do not biogenetics and Virtual Reality combined open up new 'enhanced' possibilities of *torture*, new and unheard-of horizons of extending our ability to endure pain (through widening our sensory capacity to sustain pain, through inventing new forms of inflicting it)? Perhaps the ultimate Sadeian image of an 'undead' victim of torture who can bear endless pain without having the escape into death at his or her disposal is also waiting to become reality.

The ultimate American paranoiac fantasy is that of an individual living in a small idyllic Californian city, a consumerist paradise, who suddenly starts to suspect that the world he is living in is a fake, a spectacle staged to convince him that he is living in a real world, while all the people around him are in fact actors and extras in a gigantic show. The most recent example of this is Peter Weir's *The Truman Show* (1998), with Jim Carrey playing the small-town clerk who gradually discovers the truth that he is the hero of a permanent twenty-four-hour TV show: his home town is in fact a gigantic studio set, with cameras following him everywhere. Among its predecessors, it is worth mentioning Phillip K. Dick's *Time out of Joint* (1959), in which the hero, living a modest daily life in a small idyllic Californian city in the late 1950s, gradually discovers that the whole town is a fake staged to keep him satisfied. . . . The underlying experience of *Time out of Joint* and of *The Truman Show* is that the late-capitalist consumerist Californian paradise is, in its very hyperreality, in a way *unreal*, substanceless, deprived of material inertia. And the same 'derealization' of the horror went on after the WTC collapse: while the number of victims – 3,000 – is repeated all the time, it is surprising how little of the actual carnage we see – no dismembered bodies, no blood, no desperate faces of dying people . . . in clear contrast to reporting on Third World catastrophes, where the whole point is to produce a scoop of some gruesome detail: Somalis dying of hunger, raped Bosnian women, men with their throats cut. These shots are always accompanied by an advance warning that 'some of the images you will see are extremely graphic and may upset children' – a warning which we never heard in the reports on the WTC collapse. Is this not yet further proof of how, even in this tragic moment, the distance which separates Us from Them, from their reality, is maintained: the real horror happens *there*, not *here*?[8]

So it is not only that Hollywood stages a semblance of real life

8 Another case of ideological censorship: when firefighters' widows

deprived of the weight and inertia of materiality – in late-capitalist consumerist society, 'real social life' itself somehow acquires the features of a staged fake, with our neighbours behaving in 'real' life like stage actors and extras. . . . Again, the ultimate truth of the capitalist utilitarian despiritualized universe is the dematerialization of 'real life' itself, its reversal into a spectral show. Among others, Christopher Isherwood gave expression to this unreality of American daily life, exemplified in the motel room: 'American motels are unreal! . . . They are deliberately designed to be unreal. . . . The Europeans hate us because we've retired to live inside our advertisements, like hermits going into caves to contemplate.' Peter Sloterdijk's notion of the 'sphere' is literally realized here, as the gigantic metal sphere that envelops and isolates the whole city. Years ago, a series of science-fiction films like *Zardoz* or *Logan's Run* forecast today's postmodern predicament by extending this fantasy to the community itself: the isolated group living an aseptic life in a secluded area longs for the experience of the real world of material decay. Is not the endlessly repeated shot of the plane approaching and hitting the second WTC tower the real-life version of the famous scene from Hitchcock's *Birds*, superbly analysed by Raymond Bellour, in which Melanie approaches the Bodega Bay pier after crossing the bay in a little boat? When, as she approaches the wharf, she waves to her (future) lover, a single bird (first perceived as an indistinguishable dark blot)

were interviewed on CNN, most of them gave the expected performance: tears, prayers . . . all except one who, without a tear, said that she does not pray for her dead husband, because she knows that prayer will not bring him back. Asked if she dreams of revenge, she calmly said that that would be a true betrayal of her husband: had he survived, he would have insisted that the worst thing to do is to succumb to the urge to retaliate . . . there is no need to add that this clip was shown only once, then disappeared from the repetitions of the same interviews.

unexpectedly enters the frame from above right, and hits her on the head.[9] Was not the plane which hit the WTC tower literally the ultimate Hitchcockian blot, the anamorphic stain which denaturalized the idyllic well-known New York landscape?

The Wachowski brothers' hit *Matrix* (1999) brought this logic to its climax: the material reality we all experience and see around us is a virtual one, generated and co-ordinated by a gigantic mega-computer to which we are all attached; when the hero (played by Keanu Reeves) awakens into 'real reality', he sees a desolate landscape littered with burnt-out ruins – what remains of Chicago after a global war. The resistance leader, Morpheus, utters the ironic greeting: 'Welcome to the desert of the real.' Was it not something of a similar order that took place in New York on September 11? Its citizens were introduced to the 'desert of the real' – for us, corrupted by Hollywood, the landscape and the shots of the collapsing towers could not but be reminiscent of the most breathtaking scenes in big catastrophe productions.

When we hear how the attacks were a totally unexpected shock, how the unimaginable Impossible happened, we should recall the other defining catastrophe from the beginning of the twentieth century, the sinking of the *Titanic*: this, also, was a shock, but the space for it had already been prepared in ideological fantasizing, since the *Titanic* was the symbol of the might of nineteenth-century industrial civilization. Does not the same hold also for these attacks? Not only were the media bombarding us all the time with talk about the terrorist threat; this threat was also obviously libidinally invested – just remember the series of movies from *Escape from New York* to *Independence Day*. That is the rationale of the often-mentioned association of the attacks with

9 See Chapter 3 of Raymond Bellour, *The Analysis of Film*, Bloomington: Indiana University Press 2000.

Hollywood disaster movies: the unthinkable which happened was the object of fantasy, so that, in a way, America got what it fantasized about, and that was the biggest surprise. The ultimate twist in this link between Hollywood and the 'war against terrorism' occurred when the Pentagon decided to solicit the help of Hollywood: at the beginning of October 2001, the press reported that a group of Hollywood scenarists and directors, specialists in catastrophe movies, had been established at the instigation of the Pentagon, with the aim of imagining possible scenarios for terrorist attacks and how to fight them. And this interaction seemed to be ongoing: at the beginning of November 2001, there was a series of meetings between White House advisers and senior Hollywood executives with the aim of co-ordinating the war effort and establishing how Hollywood could help in the 'war against terrorism' by getting the right ideological message across not only to Americans, but also to the Hollywood public around the globe – the ultimate empirical proof that Hollywood does in fact function as an 'ideological state apparatus'.

We should therefore invert the standard reading according to which the WTC explosions were the intrusion of the Real which shattered our illusory Sphere: quite the reverse – it was before the WTC collapse that we lived in our reality, perceiving Third World horrors as something which was not actually part of our social reality, as something which existed (for us) as a spectral apparition on the (TV) screen – and what happened on September 11 was that this fantasmatic screen apparition entered our reality. It is not that reality entered our image: the image entered and shattered our reality (i.e. the symbolic co-ordinates which determine what we experience as reality). The fact that, after September 11, the openings of many 'blockbuster' movies with scenes which bear a resemblance to the WTC collapse (tall buildings on fire or under attack, terrorist acts . . .) were postponed (or the films were even shelved) should thus be read as the 'repression' of the fantasmatic background responsible for the impact of the WTC collapse. Of course, the point is not to play a pseudo-postmodern game of reducing the WTC collapse to just another media spectacle, reading it as a catastrophe version of the snuff porno movies; the question we should have asked ourselves as we stared at the TV screens on September 11 is simply: *Where have we already seen the same thing over and over again?*

The fact that the September 11 attacks were the stuff of popular fantasies long before they actually took place provides yet another case of the twisted logic of dreams: it is easy to account for the fact that poor people around the world dream about becoming Americans – so what do the well-to-do Americans, immobilized in their well-being, dream about? About a global catastrophe that would shatter their lives – why? This is what psychoanalysis is about: to explain why, in the midst of well-being, we are haunted by nightmarish visions of catastrophes. This paradox also indicates how we should grasp Lacan's notion of 'traversing the fantasy' as the concluding moment of the psychoanalytic treatment. This notion may seem to fit perfectly the common-sense idea of what psychoanalysis should do: of course it should liberate us from the hold of idiosyncratic fantasies, and enable us to confront reality as it really is! However, this, precisely, is what Lacan does *not* have in mind – what he aims at is almost the exact opposite. In our daily existence, we are immersed in 'reality' (structured and supported by the fantasy), and this immersion is disturbed by symptoms which bear witness to the fact that another, repressed, level of our psyche resists this immersion. To 'traverse the fantasy' therefore, paradoxically, means *fully identifying oneself with the fantasy* – namely, with the fantasy which structures the excess that resists our immersion in daily reality; or, to quote a succinct formulation by Richard Boothby:

'Traversing the phantasy' thus does not mean that the subject somehow abandons its involvement with fanciful caprices and accommodates itself to a pragmatic 'reality,' but precisely the opposite: the subject is submitted to that effect of the symbolic lack that reveals the limit of everyday reality. To traverse the phantasy in the Lacanian sense is to be more profoundly claimed by the phantasy than ever, in the sense of being brought into an ever more intimate relation with that real core of the phantasy that transcends imaging.[10]

Boothby is right to emphasize the Janus-like structure of a fantasy: a fantasy is simultaneously pacifying, disarming (providing an imaginary scenario which enables us to endure the abyss of the Other's desire) *and* shattering, disturbing, inassimilable into our reality. The ideologico-political dimension of this notion of 'traversing the fantasy' was clearly revealed by the unique role the rock group *Top lista nadrealista* (*The Top List of the Surrealists*) played during the Bosnian war in the besieged town of Sarajevo: their ironic performances – which, in the midst of war and hunger, satirized the predicament of Sarajevo's population – acquired a cult status not only in the counterculture, but also among citizens of Sarajevo in general (the group's weekly TV show went on throughout the war, and was extremely popular). Instead of bemoaning the Bosnians' tragic fate, they daringly mobilized all the clichés about the 'stupid Bosnians' which were commonplace in Yugoslavia, fully identifying with them – the point thus made was that the path of true solidarity leads through direct confrontation with the obscene racist fantasies which circulated in the symbolic space of Bosnia, through playful identification with them, not

10 Richard Boothby, *Freud as Philosopher*, New York: Routledge 2001, pp. 275–6.

through the denial of these obscenities because they do not represent people as they 'really are'.

This means that the dialectic of semblance and Real cannot be reduced to the rather elementary fact that the virtualization of our daily lives, the experience that we are living more and more in an artificially constructed universe, gives rise to an irresistible urge to 'return to the Real', to regain firm ground in some 'real reality'. The Real which returns has the status of a(nother) semblance: *precisely because it is real, that is, on account of its traumatic / excessive character, we are unable to integrate it into (what we experience as) our reality, and are therefore compelled to experience it as a nightmarish apparition.* This is what the compelling image of the collapse of the WTC was: an image, a semblance, an 'effect', which, at the same time, delivered 'the thing itself'. This 'effect of the Real' is not the same as what Roland Barthes, way back in the 1960s, called *l'effet du réel*: it is, rather, its exact opposite: *l'effet de l'irréel*. That is to say: in contrast to the Barthesian *effet du réel*, in which the text makes us accept its fictional product as 'real', here, the Real itself, in order to be sustained, has to be perceived as a nightmarish unreal spectre. Usually we say that we should not mistake fiction for reality – remember the postmodern doxa according to which 'reality' is a discursive product, a symbolic fiction which we misperceive as a substantial autonomous entity. The lesson of psychoanalysis here is the opposite one: *we should not mistake reality for fiction* – we should be able to discern, in what we experience as fiction, the hard kernel of the Real which we are able to sustain only if we fictionalize it. In short, we should discern which part of reality is 'transfunctionalized' through fantasy, so that, although it is part of reality, it is perceived in a fictional mode. Much more difficult than to denounce / unmask (what appears as) reality as fiction is to recognize the part of fiction in 'real' reality. (This, of course, brings us back to the old

Lacanian notion that, while animals can deceive by presenting what is false as true, only humans (entities inhabiting the symbolic space) can deceive by presenting what is true as false.) And this insight also allows us to return to the example of cutters: if the true opposite of the Real is reality, what if, then, what they are actually escaping from when they cut themselves is not simply the feeling of unreality, of the artificial virtuality of our lifeworld, but the Real itself which explodes in the guise of uncontrolled hallucinations which start to haunt us once we lose our anchoring in reality?

Michael Haneke's *The Piano Teacher* (France/Austria 2001) helps us to negotiate this conundrum. The film is based on a short novel by Elfriede Jelinek, the story of a passionate but perverted love affair between a young pianist and his older teacher (superbly played by Isabelle Huppert): it draws on the old cliché, from *fin-de-siècle* Vienna, of a young sexually repressed girl from an upper-class family who falls passionately in love with her piano teacher. Today, however, a hundred years later, more than just the respective gender roles are reversed: in our permissive times, the affair has to be given a perverted twist. Things take a fateful turn and start to slide towards the inexorable tragic ending (the teacher's suicide) at a precise moment: when, in answer to the boy's passionate sexual advances, the 'repressed' teacher violently opens herself up to him, writing him a letter with a detailed list of her demands (basically, a scenario for masochistic performances: how he should tie her up, force her to lick his anus, slap and even beat her, and so on). It is crucial that these demands are *written* – what is put on paper is too traumatic to be pronounced in direct speech: her innermost fantasy itself.

When they are thus confronted – he with his passionate outbursts of affection and she with her cold, impassionate distance – this setting should not deceive us: it is she who in fact opens herself up, laying her fantasy bare to him, while he is simply playing a more superficial game of seduction. No wonder he withdraws in panic from her openness: the direct display of her fantasy radically changes her status in his eyes, transforming a fascinating love object into a repulsive entity he is unable to endure. Soon afterwards, however, he himself becomes perversely attracted by her fantasmatic scenario, caught up in its excessive *jouissance*, and, at first, tries to return her own message to her by enacting elements of her fantasy (he slaps her so that her nose starts to bleed, kicks her violently; when she breaks down, withdrawing from the realization of her fantasy, he passes to the act and makes love to her in order to seal his victory over her. The consummated sexual act which follows is, in its almost unbearable pain, the best exemplification of Lacan's *il n'y a pas de rapport sexuel*: although the act is performed in reality, it is – for her, at least – deprived of its fantasmatic support, and thus turns into a disgusting experience which leaves her completely cold, pushing her towards suicide. It would be totally misleading to interpret her display of fantasy as a defence-formation against the sexual act proper, as an expression of her inability to let herself go and enjoy the act: on the contrary, the displayed fantasy forms the core of her being, that which is 'in her more than herself', and it is the sexual act which is, in effect, a defence-formation against the threat embodied in the fantasy.

In his (unpublished) seminar on anxiety (1962–63), Lacan specifies that the true aim of the masochist is not to generate *jouissance* in the Other, but to provide its anxiety. That is to say: although the masochist submits himself to the Other's torture, although he wants to serve the Other, he himself defines the rules of his servitude; consequently, while he seems to offer himself as the instrument of the Other's *jouissance*, he effectively discloses his own desire to the Other and thus gives rise to anxiety in the Other – for Lacan, the true object of anxiety is precisely the (over)proximity of the Other's desire. That is the libidinal economy of the moment in *The Piano Teacher* when the heroine presents to her seducer a detailed masochistic scenario of how he should mistreat her: what repulses him is this total disclosure of her desire. (And is this not also perfectly illustrated by the painful scene from David Fincher's *Fight Club* of Ed Norton beating himself up in front of his boss? Instead of making the boss enjoy it, this spectacle obviously provokes his anxiety.)

For this reason, the true choice apropos of historical traumas is not the one between remembering or forgetting them: traumas we are not ready or able to remember haunt us all the more forcefully. We should therefore accept the paradox that, in order really to forget an event, we must first summon up the strength to remember it properly. In order to account for this paradox, we should bear in mind that the opposite of *existence* is not nonexistence, but *insistence*: that which does not exist, continues to *insist*, striving towards existence (the first to articulate this opposition was, of course, Schelling, when, in his *Treatise on Human Freedom*, he introduced the distinction between Existence and the Ground of Existence). When I miss a crucial ethical opportunity, and fail to make a move that would 'change everything', the very nonexistence of what I *should have done* will haunt me for ever: although what I did not do does not exist, its spectre continues to insist. In an outstanding reading of Walter Benjamin's 'Theses on the Philosophy of History',[11] Eric Santner elaborates Benjamin's notion that a present revolutionary intervention repeats/redeems past failed attempts: the 'symptoms' – past traces which are retroactively redeemed through the 'miracle' of the revolutionary intervention – are

11 Eric Santner, 'Miracles Happen: Benjamin, Rosenzweig, and the Limits of the Enlightenment' (unpublished paper, 2001).

'not so much forgotten deeds, but rather forgotten *failures* to act, failures to *suspend* the force of social bond inhibiting acts of solidarity with society's "others"':

> symptoms register not only past failed revolutionary attempts but, more modestly, past *failures to respond* to calls for action or even for empathy on behalf of those whose suffering in some sense belongs to the form of life of which one is a part. They hold the place of something that is *there*, that *insists* in our life, though it has never achieved full onto-logical consistency. Symptoms are thus in some sense the virtual archives of *voids* – or, perhaps, better, defenses against voids – that persist in historical experience.

Santner specifies how these symptoms can also take the form of disruptions of 'normal' social life, like participations in the obscene rituals of the reigning ideology. Was not the infamous *Kristallnacht* in 1938 – that half-organized, half-spontaneous outburst of violent attacks on Jewish homes, synagogues, busi-nesses, and people themselves – a Bakhtinian 'carnival' if ever there was one? We should read this *Kristallnacht* precisely as a 'symptom': the furious rage of such an outburst of violence makes it a symptom – the defence-formation covering up the void of the failure to intervene effectively in the social crisis. In other words, the very rage of the anti-Semitic pogroms is a proof *a contrario* of the possibility of the authentic proletarian revolution: its excessive energy can be read only as a reaction to the ('unconscious') awareness of the missed revolutionary opportunity. And is not the ultimate cause of *Ostalgie* (nostalgia for the Communist past) among many intellectuals (and even 'ordinary people') of the defunct German Democratic Republic also a longing – not so much for the Communist past, for what actually went on under Communism, but, rather, for what *might have happened* there, for the missed opportunity of another Germany? Consequently, are not post-Communist outbursts of neo-Nazi violence also a negative proof of the presence of these emancipatory chances, a symptomatic outburst of rage displaying an awareness of missed opportunities? We should not be afraid to draw a parallel with individual psychic life: just as the awareness of a missed 'private' opportunity (say, the opportunity of engaging in a fulfilling love relationship) often leaves its traces in the guise of 'irrational' anxieties, headaches, and fits of rage, the void of the missed revolutionary chance can explode in 'irrational' fits of destructive rage. . . .

Is the 'passion for the Real' as such, then, to be rejected? Definitely not, since, once we adopt this stance, the only remaining attitude is that of refusing to go to the end, of 'keeping up appearances'. The problem with the twentieth-century 'passion for the Real' was not that it was a passion for the Real, but that it was a fake passion whose ruthless pursuit of the Real behind appearances was *the ultimate stratagem to avoid confronting the Real* – how? Let us begin with the tension between universal and particular in the use of the term 'special': when we say 'We have special funds!', we mean illegal or at least secret funds, not just a special portion of public funds; when a sexual partner says 'Do you want something special?', he or she means a non-standard 'perverted' practice; when a police officer or journalist refers to 'special interrogation measures', he or she means torture or other similar illegal pressures. (And were not the units in Nazi concentration camps, which were kept apart and used for the most horrifying job of killing and cremating thousands, and disposing of the bodies, called *Sonderkommando*, special units?) In Cuba, the difficult period after the disintegration of the Eastern European Communist regimes is also referred to as the 'special period'.

Along the same lines, we should celebrate the genius of Walter Benjamin which shines through in the very title of an early work: *On Language in General and Human Language in Particular*. The point here is not that human language is a species of some universal language 'as such' which also comprises other species (language of gods and angels? animal language? the language of some other intelligent beings out there in space? computer language? the language of DNA?): there is no actually existing language other than human language – but, in order to comprehend this 'particular' language, we have to introduce a minimal difference, conceiving it in terms of the gap which separates it from language 'as such' (the pure structure of language deprived of the insignia of human finitude, erotic passions and mortality, struggles for domination and the obscenity of power). This Benjaminian lesson is the lesson missed by Habermas: what Habermas does is precisely what one should *not* do – he posits the ideal 'language in general' (pragmatic universals) *directly* as the norm for actually existing language. So, along the lines of Benjamin's title, we should describe the basic constellation of the social law as that of the 'Law in general and its obscene superego underside in particular' . . .

How does this apply to social analysis? Take Freud's analysis of the Rat Man case.[12] The Rat Man's mother had a higher social status than his father, while his father had a penchant for coarse language and a legacy of unpaid debts. Moreover, the Rat Man learned that not long before meeting his mother, his father had pursued an attractive but penniless girl, whom he abandoned to marry a rich woman. His mother's plan to marry the Rat Man into a rich family put him into the same situation as that of his father: the choice between the poor girl he loved and the more materially promising match arranged for him by his mother. It is within these co-ordinates that we should locate the fantasy of the

12 See Sigmund Freud, 'Notes Upon a Case of Obsessional Neurosis' (*Standard Edition*, Vol. 10).

rat torture (the victim is bound to a pot containing starving rats; the pot is placed upside-down on his buttocks, so that the rats gnaw their way into the victim's anus): this story was told to the Rat Man during military training. He was keen to show the regular officers that people like him (from a well-to-do-family) could nevertheless accept the rigours of army life as well as any hardened soldier of humbler birth – in this way, the Rat Man wanted to bring together the two poles of rich and poor, higher and lower social status, that had divided his family history. The cruel captain of his unit enthusiastically defended the practice of corporal punishment, and when the Rat Man disagreed with him vigorously, the captain then, as it were, threw down his trump card and described the rat torture. It is not only that the multiplicity of links which supports the terrible fascinating power of the rat-torture fantasy is sustained by the texture of signifying associations (*Rat* – advice; *Ratte* – rat; *Rate* – the interest rates to be paid; *heiraten* – to marry; *Spielratte* – a slang word for a compulsive gambler . . .). What seems crucial is the fact – rarely, if at all, mentioned by the numerous interpreters – that the choice confronted by both father and son concerns *class antagonism*: they both tried to overcome the class divide by reconciling the two opposing sides; their lot was that of a boy of humble origins who marries into a rich family, but none the less retains his ingrained low-class attitude. The figure of the cruel captain intervenes at this precise juncture: his coarse obscenity belies the idea of class reconciliation, invoking cruel bodily practices which sustain social authority. Would it not be possible to read this figure of the cruel captain as a Fascist figure of the obscene exercise of brutal power? As the cynical and brutal Fascist thug dismissing the soft-hearted liberal, aware that he is doing his dirty work for him?

Apocalypse Now Redux (2000), Francis Ford Coppola's newly edited longer version of *Apocalypse Now*, stages the co-ordinates of this structural excess of state power in the clearest possible way. Is it not significant that in the figure of Kurtz, the Freudian 'primordial father' – the obscene father-enjoyment subordinated to no symbolic Law, the total Master who dares to confront the Real of terrifying enjoyment face to face – is presented not as a remainder of some barbaric past, but as the necessary outcome of modern Western power itself? Kurtz was a perfect soldier – as such, through his overidentification with the military power system, he turned into the excess which the system has to eliminate. The ultimate horizon of *Apocalypse Now* is this insight into how Power generates its own excess, which it has to annihilate in an operation that has to imitate what it fights (Willard's mission to kill Kurtz does not exist in the official record – 'it never happened', as the general who briefs Willard points out). We thereby enter the domain of secret operations, of what the Power does without ever admitting it. And does not the same go for today's figures presented by the official media as the embodiments of radical Evil? Is this not the truth behind the fact that Bin Laden and the Taliban emerged as part of the CIA-supported anti-Soviet guerrilla movement in Afghanistan, and behind the fact that Noriega in Panama was an ex-CIA agent? Is not the USA fighting its own excess in all these cases? And was the same not true already of Fascism? The liberal West had to join forces with Communism to destroy its own excessive outgrowth. (Along the same lines, I am tempted to suggest what a truly subversive version of *Apocalypse Now* would have been: to repeat the formula of the anti-Fascist coalition, and have Willard propose to the Vietcong a pact to destroy Kurtz.) What remains outside the horizon of *Apocalypse Now* is the perspective of a collective political act *breaking out* of this vicious cycle of the System which generates its superego excess and is then compelled to annihilate it: a revolutionary violence which no longer relies on the superego obscenity. This 'impossible' act is what takes place in every authentic revolutionary process.

On the opposite side of the political field, the archetypal Eisensteinian cinematic scene which expresses the exuberant orgy of revolutionary destructive violence (what Eisenstein himself called 'a veritable bacchanalia of destruction') belongs to the same series: when, in *October*, the victorious revolutionaries penetrate the wine cellars of the Winter Palace, they indulge in an ecstatic orgy of smashing thousands of expensive wine bottles; in *Bezhin Meadow*, the village Pioneers force their way into the local church and desecrate it, robbing it of its relics, squabbling over an icon, sacrilegiously trying on vestments, laughing heretically at the statuary. . . . In this suspension of goal-orientated instrumental activity, we in effect get a kind of Bataillean 'unrestrained expenditure' – the pious desire to deprive the revolution of this excess is simply the desire to have a revolution without revolution.

This scene should be opposed to what Eisenstein does in the terrifying final scene of Part II of *Ivan the Terrible*: the carnivalesque orgy which takes place stands for the Bakhtinian fantasmatic place in which 'normal' power relations are turned around; in which the Tsar is the slave of the idiot whom he proclaims the new Tsar. In a weird mixture of Hollywood musical and Japanese theatre, the chorus of the infamous 'Oprichniki' (Ivan's private army, which has been doing his dirty work for him, mercilessly liquidating his enemies) dances and sings an utterly obscene song which celebrates the axe cutting off the heads of Ivan's enemies. The song first describes a group of boyars having a rich meal: 'Down the middle . . . the golden goblets pass . . . from hand to hand.' The Chorus then asks, with pleasurable nervous expectation: 'Come along. Come along. What happens next? Come on, tell us more!' And the solo Oprichnik, bending forward and whistling, shouts the answer: 'Strike with the axes!' Here we are at the obscene site where musical enjoyment meets political liquidation – and, taking into account the fact that the film was shot in 1944, does this not confirm the carnivalesque character of the Stalinist purges? That is the true greatness of Eisenstein: that he detected (and depicted) the fundamental shift in the status of political violence, from the 'Leninist' liberating outburst of destructive energy to the 'Stalinist' obscene underside of the Law.

The Catholic Church itself relies on (at least) two levels of such obscene unwritten rules. First, of course, there is, the infamous Opus Dei, the Church's own 'white mafia', the (half-)secret organization which somehow embodies the pure Law beyond any positive legality: its supreme rule is unconditional obedience to the Pope and a ruthless determination to work for the Church, with all other rules being (potentially) suspended. As a rule, its members, whose task is to penetrate the top political and financial circles, keep their Opus Dei identity secret. As such, they are effectively 'opus dei' – the 'work of God'; that is, they adopt the perverse position of a direct instrument of the big Other's will. Then there are the numerous cases of sexual abuse of children by priests – these cases are so widespread from Austria and Italy to Ireland and the USA, that we can in fact talk about an articulated 'counterculture' within the Church, with its set of hidden rules. And there is an interconnection between the two levels, since Opus Dei regularly intervenes to hush up sexual scandals involving priests. Incidentally, the Church's reaction to sexual scandals also demonstrates how it actually perceives its role: the Church insists that these cases, deplorable as they are, are its own internal problem, and displays great reluctance to collaborate with the police in their investigations. And, indeed, in a way, it is right: abuse of children *is* the Church's internal problem; that is to say, an inherent product of its very institutional symbolic organization, not just a series of particular criminal cases concerning individuals who happen to be priests. Consequently, the answer to this reluctance should be not only that we are dealing with criminal cases, and that if the Church does not fully participate in their investigation, it is an accessory after the fact; moreover, the Church *as such*, as an institution, should be investigated with regard to the way it systematically creates conditions for such crimes. This is also why we cannot explain the sexual scandals in which priests are involved as a manipulation by the opponents of celibacy, who want to make their point that if the priests' sexual urges do not find a legitimate outlet, they have to explode in a pathological way: allowing Catholic priests to marry would not solve anything; we would not get priests doing their job without harassing young boys, since paedophilia is generated by the Catholic institution of priesthood as its 'inherent transgression', as its obscene secret supplement.

The very core of the 'passion for the Real' is this identification with – this heroic gesture of fully assuming – the dirty obscene underside of Power: the heroic attitude of 'Somebody has to do the dirty work, so let's do it!', a kind of mirror-reversal of the Beautiful Soul which refuses to recognize itself in its result. We find this stance also in the properly Rightist admiration for the celebration of heroes who are ready to do the necessary dirty work: it is easy to do a noble thing for one's country, up to sacrificing one's life for it – it is much more difficult to commit a *crime* for one's country . . . Hitler knew very well how to play this double game apropos of the Holocaust, using Himmler to spell out the 'dirty secret'. In his speech to the SS leaders in Posen on October 4 1943, Himmler spoke quite openly about the mass killing of the Jews as 'a glorious page in our history, and one that has never been written and never can be written'; he explicitly included the killing of women and children:

WELCOME TO THE DESERT OF THE REAL!   31

> We faced the question: what should we do with the women
> and children? I decided here too to find a completely clear
> solution. I did not regard myself as justified in exterminating
> the men – that is to say, to kill them or have them killed –
> and to allow the avengers in the shape of children to grow up
> for our sons and grandchildren. The difficult decision had to
> be taken to have this people disappear from the earth.[13]

The very next day, the SS leaders were ordered to attend a
meeting where Hitler himself gave an account of the state of the
war; here, Hitler did not have to mention the Final Solution
directly – oblique references to the SS leaders' knowledge and
to their shared complicity, were enough: 'The entire German
people know that it is a matter of whether they exist or do not
exist. The bridges have been destroyed behind them. Only the
way forward remains.'[14] And, ideally, it is along these lines that
we can oppose the 'reactionary' and the 'progressive' passion for
the Real: while the 'reactionary' one is the endorsement of the
obscene underside of the Law, the 'progressive' one is confrontation with the Real of the antagonism denied by the
'passion for purification', which – in both its versions, the
Rightist and the Leftist – assumes that the Real is touched in and
through the destruction of the excessive element which intro-
duces antagonism. Here, we should abandon the standard
metaphorics of the Real as the terrifying Thing that is impossible to confront face to face, as the ultimate Real concealed
beneath the layers of imaginary and/or symbolic Veils: the very
idea that, beneath the deceptive appearances, there lies hidden
some ultimate Real Thing too horrible for us to look at directly

---

13 Quoted from Ian Kershaw, *Hitler, 1936–45: Nemesis*, Har-
   mondsworth: Penguin 2001, pp. 604–5.
14 Kershaw, *Hitler*, p. 606.

is the ultimate appearance – this Real Thing is a fantasmatic spectre whose presence guarantees the consistency of our symbolic edifice, thus enabling us to avoid confronting its constitutive inconsistency ('antagonism'). Take Nazi ideology: the Jew as its Real is a spectre evoked in order to conceal social antagonism – that is, the figure of the Jew enables us to perceive social totality as an organic Whole. And does not the same go for the figure of Woman–Thing inaccessible to the male grasp? Is she also not the ultimate Spectre enabling men to avoid the constitutive deadlock of the sexual relationship?

It is here that one should introduce the notion of *Homo sacer* recently developed by Giorgio Agamben:[15] the distinction between those who are included in the legal order and *Homo sacer* is not simply horizontal, a distinction between two groups of people, but more and more also the 'vertical' distinction between the two (superimposed) ways of how *the same* people can be treated – briefly: on the level of Law, we are treated as citizens, legal subjects, while on the level of its obscene superego supplement, of this empty unconditional law, we are treated as *Homo sacer*. Perhaps, then, the best motto for today's analysis of ideology is the line quoted by Freud at the beginning of his *Interpretation of Dreams*: *Acheronta movebo* – if you cannot change the explicit set of ideological rules, you can try to change the underlying set of obscene unwritten rules.

15 See Giorgio Agamben, *Homo Sacer*, Stanford, CA: Stanford University Press 1998.

2

REAPPROPRIATIONS: THE
LESSON OF MULLAH OMAR

Our preliminary reaction is that the shattering impact of the
September 11 attacks can be accounted for only against the
background of the border which today separates the digitalized
First World from the Third World 'desert of the Real'. It is the
awareness that we live in an insulated artificial universe which
generates the notion that some ominous agent is threatening us
all the time with total destruction. In this paranoiac perspective,
the terrorists are turned into an irrational abstract agency –
abstract in the Hegelian sense of subtracted from the concrete
socio-ideological network which gave birth to it. Every explanation which evokes social circumstances is dismissed as covert
justification of terror, and every particular entity is evoked only
in a negative way: the terrorists betray the true spirit of Islam,
they do not express the interests and hopes of the poor Arab
masses. . . . In the days after September 11, the media reported
that not only English translations of the Koran but also books
about Islam and Arab culture in general became instant best-
sellers: people wanted to understand what Islam is, and it is safe
to surmise that the vast majority of those who wanted to understand Islam were not anti-Arab racists, but people eager to give

Islam a chance, to get a feel for it, to experience it from the inside, and thus to redeem it – their desire was to convince themselves that Islam is a great spiritual force which cannot be blamed for the terrorist crimes. Sympathetic as this attitude may be (and what can be ethically more appealing than, in the midst of a violent confrontation, trying to put oneself inside the opponent's mind, and thus to relativize one's own standpoint?), it remains a gesture of ideological mystification *par excellence*: probing into different cultural traditions is precisely *not* the way to grasp the political dynamics which led to the September 11 attacks. Is not the fact that Western leaders, from Bush to Netanyahu and Sharon, repeat like a mantra how Islam is a great religion, which has nothing to do with the horrible crimes committed in its name, a clear sign that something about this praise is wrong? When, in October 2001, the Italian Prime Minister, Silvio Berlusconi, made his famous 'slip of the tongue' and, to the consternation of Western liberals, claimed that human rights and freedoms emerged from the Christian tradition, which is clearly superior to Islam, his stance was, in a way, much more to the point than other leaders' disgustingly patronizing liberal respect for the Other's spiritual depth.

Recently, comments like 'The End of the Age of Irony' have abounded in our media, pushing home the notion that the age of a postmodern deconstructive sliding of sense is over: now once again we need firm and unambiguous commitments. Unfortunately, Jürgen Habermas himself (in his speech of acceptance upon receiving the German publishers' prize in October 2001) joined this chorus, emphasizing that postmodern relativism's time is over. (If anything, the events of September 11 indicate the utter impotence of Habermasian ethics – should we say that there is 'distorted communication' between Muslims and the liberal West?) Along the same lines, Rightist commentators like George Will also immediately proclaimed the end of the American 'holiday from history' – the impact of reality shattering the isolated tower of the liberal tolerant attitude and the Cultural Studies focus on textuality. Now, we are forced to strike back, to deal with real enemies in the real world. . . . However, *whom* do we strike? Whatever the response, it will never hit the right target, bringing us full satisfaction. The ridicule of America attacking Afghanistan is a case in point: if the greatest power in the world bombards one of the poorest countries, in which peasants barely survive on barren hills, is this not the ultimate case of impotent acting out? Afghanistan is otherwise an ideal target: a country that is already reduced to rubble, with no infrastructure, repeatedly destroyed by war for the last two decades. . . . We cannot avoid the surmise that the choice of Afghanistan was also determined by economic considerations: is it not the best procedure to act out one's anger at a country for which no one cares and where there is nothing to destroy? Unfortunately, the choice of Afghanistan cannot fail to recall the anecdote about the madman who searches for a lost key beneath a streetlamp; asked why there, when he lost the key in a dark corner, he answers: 'But it's easier to search under a strong light!' Is not the ultimate irony that prior to the US bombing, the whole of Kabul already looked like downtown Manhattan after September 11? The 'war on terrorism' thus functions as an act whose true aim is to lull us into the falsely secure conviction that nothing has really changed.

It is already a journalistic cliché that a new form of war is now emerging: a high-tech war in which precision bombing, and so on, does the job, without any direct intervention by ground forces (if they are needed at all, this job can be left to 'local allies'). Old notions of face-to-face combat, courage, and so on, are becoming obsolete. We should note the structural homology between this new warfare-at-a-distance, where the 'soldier' (a computer specialist) pushes buttons hundreds of miles away, and the decisions of managerial bodies which affect millions (IMF specialists dictating the conditions a Third World country has to meet in order to deserve financial aid; WTO regulations; corporate boards deciding about necessary 'restructuring'): in both cases, abstraction is inscribed into a very 'real' situation – decisions are made which will affect thousands, sometimes causing terrifying havoc and destruction, but the link between these 'structural' decisions and the painful reality of millions is broken; the 'specialists' taking the decisions are unable to imagine the consequences, since they measure the effects of these decisions in abstract terms (a country can be 'financially sane' even if millions in it are starving).

And today's 'terrorism' is simply the counterpoint to this warfare. The true long-term threat is further acts of mass terror in comparison with which the memory of the WTC collapse will pale – acts that are less spectacular, but much more horrifying. What about bacteriological warfare, what about the use of lethal gas, what about the prospect of DNA terrorism (developing poisons which will affect only people who share a specific genome)? In contrast to Marx, who relied on the notion of the fetish as a solid object whose stable presence obfuscates its social mediation, we should assert that fetishism reaches its acme precisely when the fetish itself is 'dematerialized', turned into a fluid 'immaterial' virtual entity; money fetishism will culminate with the passage to its electronic form, when the last traces of its materiality have disappeared – it is only at this stage that it will assume the form of an indestructible spectral presence: I owe you 1,000 dollars, and no matter how many material notes I burn, I still owe you 1,000 dollars – the debt is inscribed somewhere in virtual digital space. . . . Does not the same also hold for warfare? Far from pointing towards the twentieth-century warfare, the WTC twin towers explosion and collapse in September 2001 were, rather, the last spectacular cry of twentieth-century warfare. What awaits us is something much more uncanny: the spectre of an 'immaterial' war where the attack is invisible – viruses, poisons which can be anywhere and nowhere. On the level of visible material reality, nothing happens, no big explosions; yet the known universe starts to collapse, life disintegrates.

We are entering a new era of paranoiac warfare in which the greatest task will be to identify the enemy and his weapons. In this new warfare, the agents assume their acts less and less publicly: not only are 'terrorists' themselves no longer eager to claim responsibility for their acts (even the notorious al-Qaeda did not explicitly appropriate the September 11 attacks, not to mention the mystery about the origins of the anthrax letters); 'antiterrorist' state measures themselves are clouded in a shroud of secrecy – all this forming an ideal breeding-ground for conspiracy theories and generalized social paranoia.

And is not the obverse of this paranoiac omnipresence of the invisible war its desubstantialization? Just as we drink beer without alcohol or coffee without caffeine, we are now getting war deprived of its substance – a virtual war fought behind computer screens, a war experienced by its participants as a video game, a war with no casualties (on our side, at least). With the spread of the anthrax panic in October 2001, the West got the first taste of this new 'invisible' warfare in which – an aspect we should always bear in mind – we, ordinary citizens, are totally dependent on the authorities for information about what is going on: we see and hear nothing; all we know comes from the official media. A superpower bombing a desolate desert country and, at the same time, hostage to invisible bacteria – this, not the WTC explosions, is the first image of twenty-first-century warfare. Instead of a quick acting out, we should confront some difficult questions: what will 'war' mean in the twenty-first century? Who will 'they' be if they are,

clearly, neither states nor criminal gangs? Here I cannot resist
the temptation to recall the Freudian opposition of the public
Law and its obscene superego double: along the same lines, are
not 'international terrorist organizations' the obscene double of
the big multinational corporations – the ultimate rhizomatic
machine, omnipresent, albeit with no clear territorial base? Are
they not the form in which nationalist and/or religious 'fundamentalism' accommodated itself to global capitalism? Do they
not embody the ultimate contradiction, with their particu-
lar/exclusive content and their global dynamic functioning?

An emblematic (post-) Yugoslav Serb film, *Pretty Village,
Pretty Flame* (Srdjan Dragojevič, 1996), somehow prefigures this
shift in the figure of the Enemy.[16] The story takes place during
the first winter of the Bosnian war, when a group of Serb army
fighters are trapped by Bosnian soldiers in a deserted railway
tunnel; between outbreaks of fighting, the soldiers inside and
outside the tunnel provoke each other by exchanging nationalist insults. The key feature of the narrative, however, is that this
stand-off between the two sides involved in the conflict, which
lasts for ten days, is presented entirely from the perspective of
those inside the tunnel, the Serb fighters; until the very final
dénouement, the 'Muslim side' is presented only as an assem-
blage of what Michel Chion called 'acousmatic voices'; vulgar
insults or wild half-animal shouting which are not (yet) attributed to particular visually identified individuals, and thus acquire
an all-powerful spectral dimension.[17] The narrative device thus
mobilized is, of course, taken from many horror films, and even
Westerns, in which a group of sympathetic characters is encir-
cled by an invisible Enemy who is mainly heard and seen only in

16 I rely here on Pavle Levi's outstanding doctoral thesis
   'Disintegration in Frames' (New York University 2002).
17 See Michel Chion, *The Voice in Cinema*, New York: Columbia
   University Press 2000.

the guise of fleeting shadows and blurred appearances (from Jacques Tourneur's underrated Western *Apache Drums* to John Carpenter's *Assault on Precinct 13*).[18]

This very formal device compels us, the spectators, to identify with the besieged Serb group, and the fact that Serb soldiers are offered as the viewer's point of identification is further confirmed by a strange feature: although, at the beginning of the film, we see Muslim villages destroyed by violently rampaging Serb soldiers, these soldiers are not those who are later trapped in the tunnel; these soldiers mysteriously just pass through burnt-out villages – no killing seems to take place, no one seems to die . . . This properly fetishist split (although we, the spectators, know very well that these soldiers must have done their share of killing Muslim civilians, we are not shown this, so that we can continue to believe that their hands are not full of blood) creates the conditions for our sympathetic identification with them. In contrast to the Muslims – an unidentified spectral Entity of insults, threats and wild shouts – the Serbs are thus fully individualized, basically characterized as a bunch of 'crazy but sympathetic' antiheroes. And, as Pavle Levi remarks perspicaciously, the potential subversive dimension of this device (if the Enemy is purely acousmatic, and thus spectral, what if it is just a paranoiac projection of the Serbs themselves, the result of

---

18 This implicit reference to Westerns is even more complex, since the film *turns around* the usual perception of Bosnians as the besieged city-dwellers and Serbs as the attacking besiegers starving out a large city (Sarajevo, exemplarily): here, the Serbs are the besieged ones and the Bosnians the attacking besiegers. (And, incidentally, it is Peter Handke who, in his defence of the Serbs, refers to this cliché, giving it a Politically Correct twist: since we know today that Indians (Native Americans) were the 'good guys' defending their country from the invading European colonizers, should we not draw the same conclusion apropos of the Bosnian war and support the Serbs, who here play the role of the Native Americans?)

their ideological imagination?) is undercut by the 'désacous-matisation' at the end, when Halil, the key Muslim soldier, is fully shown and identified as the childhood best friend of Milan, the main Serb character.

Do not these examples illustrate the notorious 'clash of civilizations' thesis? There is, of course, a partial truth in this notion – witness the surprise of the average American: 'How is it possible that these people display and practise such a disregard for their own lives?' Is not the obverse of this surprise the rather sad fact that we, in First World countries, find it more and more difficult even to imagine a public or universal Cause for which we would be ready to sacrifice our life? When, after the bombings, even the Taliban Foreign Minister said that he could 'feel the pain' of the American children, did he not thereby confirm the hegemonic ideological role of Bill Clinton's trademark phrase? It does seem as if the split between First World and Third World runs more and more along the lines of the opposition between leading a long and satisfying life full of material and cultural wealth, and dedicating one's life to some transcendent Cause.

Two philosophical references immediately suggest themselves apropos of this ideological antagonism between the Western consumerist way of life and Muslim radicalism: Hegel and Nietzsche. Is not this antagonism the one between what Nietzsche called 'passive' and 'active' nihilism? We in the West are the Nietzschean Last Men, immersed in stupid daily pleasures, while the Muslim radicals are ready to risk everything, engaged in the struggle even up to their own self-destruction. (We cannot fail to note the significant role of the stock exchange in the attacks: the ultimate proof of their traumatic impact was that the New York Stock Exchange was closed for four days, and its opening the following Monday was presented as the key sign that things were returning to normal.) Furthermore, if we look at this opposition through the lens of the Hegelian struggle between Master and Servant, we cannot avoid a paradox: although we in the West are perceived as exploiting masters, it is we who occupy the position of the Servant who, since he clings to life and its pleasures, is unable to risk his life (recall Colin Powell's notion of a high-tech war with no human casualties), while the poor Muslim radicals are Masters ready to risk their life . . . This notion of the 'clash of civilizations', however, must be rejected out of hand: what we are witnessing today are, rather, clashes *within* each civilization. Furthermore, a brief look at the comparative history of Islam and Christianity tells us that the 'human rights record' of Islam (to use this anachronistic term) is much better than that of Christianity: in past centuries, Islam has been significantly more tolerant towards other religions than Christianity. Now it is also time to remember that it was through the Arabs that, in the Middle Ages, we in Western Europe regained access to our Ancient Greek heritage. While they in no way excuse today's acts of horror, these facts none the less clearly demonstrate that we are dealing not with a feature inscribed into Islam 'as such', but with the outcome of modern sociopolitical conditions.

If we look more closely, what is this 'clash of civilizations' actually about? Are not all real-life 'clashes' clearly related to global capitalism? The Muslim 'fundamentalist' target is not only global capitalism's corrosive impact on social life, but also the corrupt 'traditionalist' regimes in Saudi Arabia, Kuwait, and so on. The most horrifying slaughters (those in Rwanda, Kongo, and Sierra Leone) not only took place – and are still taking place – within the same 'civilization', but are also clearly related to the interplay of global economic interests. Even in the few cases which would vaguely fit the definition of the 'clash of civilizations' (Bosnia and Kosovo, southern Sudan, etc.), the shadow of other interests is easily discernible. A proper dose of 'economic reductionism' would therefore be appropriate here: instead of endless analyses of how Islamic 'fundamentalism' is intolerant towards our liberal societies, and other 'clash-of-civilization' topics, we should refocus our attention on the economic background to the conflict – the clash of *economic* interests, and of the geopolitical interests of the United States itself (how to retain privileged links with Israel and with conservative Arab regimes like those of Saudi Arabia and Kuwait).

Beneath the opposition between 'liberal' and 'fundamentalist' societies, 'McWorld versus Jihad', there is the embarrassing third term: countries like Saudi Arabia and Kuwait, deeply conservative monarchies but American economic allies, fully integrated into Western capitalism. Here, the USA has a very precise and simple interest: in order that these countries can be counted on for their oil reserves, they have to remain undemocratic (the underlying notion, of course, is that any democratic awakening could give rise to anti-American attitudes). This is an old story whose infamous first chapter after World War II was the CIA-orchestrated *coup d'état* against Iran's democratically elected Prime Minister, Hedayat Mossadegh, in 1953 – there was no 'fundamentalism' there, not even a 'Soviet threat', just a plain democratic awakening, with the idea that the country should take control of its oil resources and break up the monopoly of the Western oil companies. The lengths to which the USA is ready to go in order to maintain this pact were revealed in the Gulf War in 1990, when Jewish American soldiers stationed in Saudi Arabia had to be transported by helicopter to aircraft carriers in the Gulf in order to pray, since non-Muslim rituals are prohibited on Saudi soil.

This 'perverted' position of the truly 'fundamentalist' conservative Arab regimes is the key to the (often comical) conundrums of American politics in the Middle East: they stand for the point at which the USA is forced explicitly to acknowledge the primacy of economy over democracy – that is, the secondary and manipulative character of legitimizing international interventions – by claiming to protect democracy and human rights. What we should always bear in mind apropos of Afghanistan is that until the 1970s – that is, prior to the time when the country got directly caught up in the superpower struggle – it was one of the most tolerant Muslim societies, with a long secular tradition: Kabul was known as a city with a vibrant cultural and political life. The paradox is thus that the rise of the Taliban, this apparent 'regresion' into ultra-fundamentalism, far from expressing some deep 'traditionalist' tendency, was the result of the country being caught up in the whirlpool of international politics – it was not only a defensive reaction to it, it emerged directly as a result of the support of foreign powers (Pakistan, Saudi Arabia, the USA itself).

As for the 'clash of civilizations', let us recall the letter from the seven-year-old American girl whose father was a pilot fighting in Afghanistan: she wrote that – although she loved her father very much, she was ready to let him die, to sacrifice him for her country. When President Bush quoted these lines, they were perceived as a 'normal' outburst of American patriotism; let us conduct a simple mental experiment and imagine an Arab Muslim girl pathetically reciting into the camera the same words about her father fighting for the Taliban – we do not have to think for long about what our reaction would have been: morbid Muslim fundamentalism which does not stop even at the cruel manipulation and exploitation of children. . . . Every feature attributed to the Other is already present at the very heart of the USA. Murderous fanaticism? There are in the USA today more than two million Rightist populist 'fundamentalists' who also practise a terror of their own, legitimized by (their understanding of) Christianity. Since America is, in a way, 'harbouring' them, should the US Army have punished Americans themselves after the Oklahoma bombing? And what about the way Jerry Falwell and Pat Robertson reacted to the events of September 11, perceiving them as a sign that God had withdrawn His protection from the USA because of the sinful lives of the Americans, putting the blame on hedonist materialism, liberalism, and rampant sexuality, and claiming that America got what it deserved? The fact that this very same condemnation of 'liberal' America as the one from the Muslim Other came from the very heart of *l'Amérique profonde* should give us food for thought. On October 19, George W. Bush himself had to concede that the most probable perpetrators of the anthrax attacks were not Muslim terrorists but America's own extreme Right Christian fundamentalists – again, does not the fact that acts first attributed to an external enemy may turn out to be acts perpetrated at the very heart of *l'Amérique profonde* provide an unexpected confirmation of the thesis that the true clash is the clash within each civilization?[19]

Now, in the months following the attacks, it is as if we are living in the unique time between a traumatic event and its symbolic impact, as in those brief moments after we have been deeply cut, before the full extent of the pain strikes us. We do not yet know how the events will be symbolized, what their symbolic efficiency will be, what acts they will be

---

19 According to some conservative US lawyers, an act done out of religious conviction cannot by definition be insane, since religion stands for the highest spiritual dimension of humanity. How, then, are we to categorize the Palestinian suicide bombers? Is their religious belief authentic or not? If not, can the same insanity label be applied to homegrown American Christian terrorists? This is the old Enlightenment topic of the fragile border between religion and madness, or religious 'superstition' and pure 'rational' religion.

evoked to justify. If nothing else, we can clearly experience yet again the limitations of our democracy: decisions are being made which will affect the fate of all of us, and all of us just wait, aware that we are utterly powerless. In the aftermath of September 11 the Americans *en masse* rediscovered their American pride, displaying flags and singing together in public, but I should emphasize more than ever that there is nothing 'innocent' about this rediscovery of American innocence, about getting rid of the sense of historical guilt or irony which prevented many Americans from fully assuming their national identity. What this gesture amounted to was 'objectively' assuming the burden of all that being 'American' stood for in the past – an exemplary case of ideological interpellation, of fully assuming one's symbolic mandate, which comes on the scene after the perplexity caused by some historical trauma. In the traumatic aftermath of September 11, when the old security seemed to be momentarily shattered, what could be more 'natural' than taking refuge in the innocence of a firm ideological identification?[20] However, it is precisely such moments of transparent innocence, of 'back to basics', when the gesture of identification seems 'natural', that are, from the standpoint of the critique of ideology, the most obscure – even, in a certain way, obscurity itself.

Let us recall another such innocently transparent moment, the endlessly reproduced video shot from Beijing's Avenue of Eternal Peace, at the height of the 'troubles' in 1989, of a tiny young man with a can who, alone, stands in front of an advancing gigantic tank, and courageously tries to prevent its advance, so that, when the tank tries to go round him by turning right or

---

20 Here I draw on my critical elaboration of Althusser's notion of interpellation in Chapter 3 of *Metastases of Enjoyment,* London and New York: Verso 1995.

left, the man also moves aside, again standing in its way: 'The representation is so powerful that it demolishes all other understandings. This street scene, this time and this event, have come to constitute the compass point for virtually all Western journeys into the interior of the contemporary political and cultural life of China.'[21]

Again, this very moment of transparent clarity (things are presented in their utmost nakedness: a lone man against the brute force of the State) is, for our Western gaze, sustained by a cobweb of ideological implications, embodying a series of oppositions: individual versus state; peaceful resistance versus state violence; man versus machine; the inner force of a tiny individual versus the impotence of the powerful machine. . . . These implications, against the background of which the shot exerts its full direct impact, these 'mediations' which sustain the shot's immediate impact, are not present for a Chinese observer, since such a series of oppositions is inherent to the European ideological legacy. And the same ideological background also overdetermines, say, our perception of the horrifying images of tiny individuals jumping from the burning WTC tower to certain death.

So what about the phrase which reverberates everywhere: 'Nothing will ever be the same after September 11'? Significantly, this phrase is never further elaborated – it is just an empty gesture of saying something 'deep' without really knowing what we want to say. So our first reaction to it should be: Really? What if, precisely, nothing epochal happened on September 11? What if – as the massive display of American patriotism seems to demonstrate – the shattering experience of

21 Michael Dutton, *Streetlife China*, Cambridge: Cambridge University Press 1998, p. 17.

September 11 ultimately served as a device which enabled the hegemonic American ideology to 'go back to its basics', to reassert its basic ideological co-ordinates against the antiglobalist and other critical temptations? Perhaps I should none the less qualify this statement by introducing the temporality of *futur antérieur*: on September 11, the USA was given the opportunity to realize what kind of world it was part of. It might have taken this opportunity – but it did not; instead it opted to reassert its traditional ideological commitments: out with feelings of responsibility and guilt towards the impoverished Third World, *we* are the victims now! So when, apropos of the Hague Tribunal, Timothy Garton Ash pathetically claims: 'No Führer or Duce, no Pinochet, no Idi Amin and no Pol Pot should any longer be allowed to feel safe from the intervention of the people's justice behind the palace gates of sovereignty',[22] we should simply take note of who is *missing* in this series of names which, apart from the standard couple of Hitler and Mussolini, contains three Third World dictators: where is at least one name from the Big Seven – say, somebody like Kissinger?

Consider the collapse of a political regime – say, the collapse of the Communist regimes in Eastern Europe in 1990: at a certain moment, people became aware all of a sudden that the game was over, that the Communists had lost. The break was purely symbolic; nothing changed 'in reality' – none the less, from that moment on, the final collapse of the regime was merely a matter of days away. . . . What if something of the same order *did* occur on 11 September? Perhaps the ultimate victim of the WTC collapse will be a certain figure of the big Other, the American Sphere. During Nikita Khrushchev's secret speech at the Twentieth Congress of the Soviet Party,

22 Timothy Garton Ash, 'Slobo und Carla', *Sueddeutsche Zeitung*, 14 March 2002, p. 15 (my translation).

denouncing Stalin's crimes, a dozen or so delegates suffered nervous breakdowns and had to be carried out and given medical help; one of them, Boleslaw Bierut, the hardline General Secretary of the Polish Communist Party, even died of a heart attack a few days later. (And the model Stalinist writer Alexander Fadeyev shot himself a few days later.) The point is not that they were 'honest Communists' – most of them were brutal manipulators without any subjective illusions about the nature of the Soviet regime. What broke down was their 'objective' illusion, the figure of the 'big Other' against the background of which they could exert their ruthless drive for power: the Other on to which they transposed their belief, the Other which, as it were, believed on their behalf, their subject-supposed-to-believe, disintegrated. And did not something analogous happen in the aftermath of September 11? Was not September 11 2001 the Twentieth Congress of the American Dream?

September 11 is already being appropriated for ideological causes: from the claims in all the mass media that antiglobalization is now out, to the notion that the shock of the WTC attacks revealed the substanceless character of postmodern Cultural Studies, their lack of contact with 'real life'. While the second notion is (partially) right for the wrong reasons, the first is downright wrong. What is true is that the relatively trifling character of standard Cultural Studies critical topics was thereby revealed: what is the use of a politically incorrect expression with possible racist undertones, compared with the torturous death of thousands? This is the dilemma of Cultural Studies: will they stick to the same topics, directly admitting that their fight against oppression is a fight within First World capitalism's universe – which means that, in the wider conflict between the Western First World and the outside threat to it, one should reassert one's fidelity to the basic American liberal-democratic framework? Or will they risk taking the step into radicalizing their critical stance; will they problematize this framework itself? As for the end of antiglobalization, the dark hints from the first days after September 11 that the attacks could also have been the work of antiglobalist terrorists is, of course, nothing but a crude manipulation: the only way to conceive of what happened on September 11 is to locate it in the context of the antagonisms of global capitalism.

We do not yet know what consequences this event will have for the economy, ideology, politics and war, but one thing is certain: the USA, which, until now, perceived itself as an island exempt from this kind of violence, witnessing it only from the safe distance of the TV screen, is now directly involved. So the alternative is: will the Americans decide to fortify their 'sphere' further, or to risk stepping out of it? Either America will persist in – even strengthen the deeply immoral attitude of 'Why should this happen to us? Things like this don't happen *here*!', leading to more aggressivity towards the threatening Outside – in short: to a paranoiac acting out. Or America will finally risk stepping through the fantasmatic screen that separates it from the Outside World, accepting its arrival in the Real world, making the long-overdue move from 'A thing like this shouldn't happen *here*!' to 'A thing like this shouldn't happen *anywhere*!'. That is the true lesson of the attacks: the only way to ensure that it will not happen here again is to prevent it happening anywhere else. In short, America should learn humbly to accept its own vulnerability as part of this world, enacting the punishment of those responsible as a sad duty, not as an exhilarating retaliation – what we are getting instead is the forceful reassertion of the exceptional role of the USA as a global policeman, as if what causes resentment against the USA is not its excess of power, but its lack of it.

The WTC attacks confront us with the necessity of resisting

the temptation of a double blackmail. If we simply, only and unconditionally condemn it, we simply appear to endorse the blatantly ideological position of American innocence under attack by Third World Evil; if we draw attention to the deeper sociopolitical causes of Arab extremism, we simply appear to blame the victim which ultimately got what it deserved. . . . The only possible solution here is to reject this very opposition and to adopt both positions simultaneously; this can be done only if we resort to the dialectical category of totality: there is no choice between these two positions; each one is one-sided and false. Far from offering a case apropos of which we can adopt a clear ethical stance, we encounter here the limit of moral reasoning: from the moral standpoint, the victims are innocent, the act was an abominable crime, this very innocence, however, is not innocent – to adopt such an 'innocent' position in today's global capitalist universe is in itself a false abstraction. The same goes for the more ideological clash of interpretations: we can claim that the attack on the WTC was an attack on everything that is worth fighting for in democratic freedoms – the decadent Western way of life condemned by Muslim and other fundamentalists is the universe of women's rights and multiculturalist tolerance;[23] we could also claim, however, that it was an attack on the very centre and symbol of global financial capitalism. This, of course, in no way entails the compromise notion of shared guilt (the terrorists are to blame, but the Americans are also partly to blame . . .) – the point is, rather, that the two sides are not really opposed; that they belong to the

23 Along these lines, recall the Taliban Foreign Minister's answer, to a Western journalists' question: why do women in Afghanistan not play a greater role (or, rather, *any* role) in public affairs? 'How can you trust a person who bleeds on her own every month for a couple of days!'

same field. In short, the position to adopt is to accept the necessity of the fight against terrorism, but to redefine and expand its terms so that it will also include (some) American and other Western powers' acts: the choice between Bush and Bin Laden is not our choice; they are both 'Them' against Us. The fact that global capitalism is a totality means that it is the dialectical unity of itself and of its other, of the forces which resist it on 'fundamentalist' ideological grounds.

Consequently, of the two main stories which emerged after September 11, both are worse, as Stalin would have put it. The American patriotic narrative – the innocence under siege, the surge of patriotic pride – is, of course, vain; however, is the Leftist narrative (with its *Schadenfreude*: the USA got what it deserved, what it had been doing to others for decades) really any better? The predominant reaction of European – but also American – Leftists was nothing less than scandalous: all imaginable stupidities were said and written, up to the 'feminist' point that the WTC towers were two phallic symbols, waiting to be destroyed ('castrated'). Was there not something petty and miserable in the mathematics reminding us of Holocaust revisionism (what are the 3,000 dead against millions in Rwanda, Kongo, etc.)? And what about the fact that the CIA (co-)created the Taliban and Bin Laden, financing and helping them to fight the Soviets in Afghanistan? Why was this fact quoted as an argument against attacking them? Would it not be much more logical to claim that it is precisely America's duty to rid us of the monster it created? The moment we think in the terms of 'Yes, the WTC collapse was a tragedy, but we should not fully solidarize with the victims, since this would mean supporting US imperialism', the ethical catastrophe is already here: the only appropriate stance is unconditional solidarity with *all* victims. The ethical stance proper is replaced here by the moralizing mathematics of guilt and horror, which misses the key point: the terrifying death of each individual is absolute and incomparable. In short, let us conduct a simple mental experiment: if you detect in yourself any reluctance to empathize fully with the victims of the WTC collapse, if you feel the urge to qualify your empathy with 'Yes, but what about the millions who suffer in Africa . . .', you are not demonstrating your Third World sympathies, but merely the *mauvaise foi* which bears witness to your implicit patronizing racist attitude towards Third World victims. (More precisely, the problem with such comparative statements is that they are both necessary and inadmissible: one *has* to make them, one *has* to make the point that much worse horrors are taking place around the world on a daily basis – but one has to do it without getting involved in the obscene mathematics of guilt.)

One of the current Leftist wisdoms is best exemplified by the image on the cover of the Verso catalogue for spring 2002: George Bush as a Muslim cleric with a beard – the global capitalist liberalism which opposes Muslim fundamentalism is itself a mode of fundamentalism, so that, in the current 'war on terrorism', we are in effect dealing with a clash of fundamentalisms. Despite its rhetorical efficiency, this *doxa* obfuscates the opposite – much more unsettling – paradox: the Muslim fundamentalists are not true fundamentalists, they are already 'modernists', a product and a phenomenon of modern global capitalism – they stand for the way the Arab world strives to accommodate itself to global capitalism. We should therefore also reject the standard liberal wisdom according to which Islam still needs to accomplish the Protestant revolution which would open it up to modernity: this Protestant revolution was already accomplished more than two centuries ago, in the guise of the Wahhabi movement which emerged in (what is today) Saudi Arabia. Its basic tenet, the exercise of *ijtihad* (the right to reinterpret Islam on the basis of changing conditions), is the precise counterpart to Luther's reading of the Bible. *Ijtihad* is a properly dialectical notion: neither a spontaneous immersion in old traditions nor the need to 'adapt to new conditions' and compromise, but the urge to *reinvent eternity itself* in new historical conditions. The Wahhabis were extremely 'purist' and 'dogmatic', opposed to any kind of cheap accommodation to new trends of Western modernity; and, simultaneously, they advocated the ruthless abandonment of old superstitious organic mores – the very formula of the 'Protestant' return to origins against the corrupting inertia of tradition.

Another way in which the Left miserably failed is that, in the weeks after the attacks, it reverted to the old mantra 'Give peace a chance! War does not stop violence!' – a true case of hysterical precipitation, reacting to something which will not even happen in the expected form. Instead of a concrete analysis of the new complex situation after the attacks, of the chances it gives the Left to propose its own interpretation of the events, we got the blind ritualistic chant 'No war!', which fails to address even the elementary fact, *de facto* acknowledged by the US government itself (through its postponing of the retaliatory action for a month), that this is not a war like others, that the bombing of Afghanistan is not a solution. A sad situation, in which George Bush showed more power of reflection than most of the Left! Yet another false Leftist argument was that the perpetrators of the WTC attacks should be persecuted and treated as criminals – what happened was a criminal act. This notion completely misses the political dimension of today's 'terrorism'.[24]

24 When we are dealing with today's Left, we should also always bear in mind the Leftist narcissism for the lost Cause, best characterized as the inversion of Talleyrand's well-known cynicism: when, while at dinner, he overheard the sounds of a street battle, he commented to his companions at the table: 'You see, our side is winnng!' Asked 'Which side?', he answered: 'We'll know tomorrow, when we find out who won!' The Leftist nostalgic's attitude is: 'You see, our side is losing!' 'Which side?' 'We'll know that tomorrow, when we find out who lost!'

With such a 'Left', who needs the Right? No wonder, then, that in the face of such 'Leftist' follies, the ease with which the hegemonic ideology appropriated the September 11 tragedy and imposed its basic message was even greater than one might expect given that the mainstream Right and Liberal Centre control the mass media: the easy games are over now, we should take sides – against or for (terrorism). And since nobody is openly for, this means that doubt itself, a questioning attitude, is denounced as covert support for terrorism. . . . This, precisely, is the temptation to be resisted: *precisely in such moments of apparent clarity of choice, mystification is total*. The choice proposed to us is not the true choice. Today, more than ever, we should summon up the strength to step back and reflect upon the background of the situation. Intellectuals who succumbed to temptation are exemplified by the group of fifty who, in February 2002, signed the ridiculous appeal to American patriotism – a clear case of the pragmatic paradox of self-cancelling designation (the intellectuals who signed that appeal thereby irrevocably lost their status as intellectuals).

First complication: is the crucial choice today really that of liberal democracy versus fundamentalism or its derivations (like modernization versus resistance to it)? The only way to account for the complexity and the strange twists of today's global situation is to insist that the true choice is the one between capitalism and its Other (at this moment represented by marginal currents like the antiglobalization movement); this choice is then accompanied by phenomena which are structurally secondary, crucial among them the inherent tension between capitalism and its own excess. Throughout the twentieth century, the same pattern is clearly discernible: in order to crush its true enemy, capitalism started to play with fire, and mobilized its obscene excess in the guise of Fascism; this excess, however, took on a life of its own, and became so strong that mainstream 'liberal' capitalism had to join forces with its true enemy (Communism) to subdue it. Significantly, the war between capitalism and Communism was a cold one, while the big Hot War was fought against Fascism. And is not the case of the Taliban the same? After their ghost was concocted to fight Communism, they turned into the main enemy. Consequently, even if terrorism burns us all, the US 'war on terrorism' is not our struggle, but a struggle internal to the capitalist universe. The first duty of a progressive intellectual (if this term has any meaning left in it today) is not to fight the enemy's struggles for him.

Second complication: we should 'deconstruct' Afghanistan itself; it never existed 'in itself', it was the creation of outside forces from the very beginning. If we follow the 'natural' lines of ethnic division, then the northern and western parts of Afghanistan should have been included in the ex-Soviet Muslim republics (Tajikistan, Uzbekistan) or Iran; while the west and south, together with the northeast of Pakistan, should form a Pashtun state of its own (the Pashtuns are split around 50/50 between Afghanistan and Pakistan). And what about the weird wormlike protuberance on the northeast, populated by Tajiks? It was artificially carved out a hundred years ago as a buffer zone, to prevent direct contact between British and Russian domains. At the same time, the Pashtun area was split by the arbitrary Durand Line to prevent the Pashtuns from threatening British interests in Pakistan (then India). (And it would be easy to show that the same goes for Pakistan itself – a land with no tradition of its own, an artificial entity if ever there was one.)

So, far from being an ancient realm outside the scope of modernization, until recently untouched by history, *the very existence of Afghanistan is the result of the interplay of foreign powers*. The closest one can get to Afghanistan in Europe would be something like Belgium: a buffer zone between France and the Netherlands which originated in the war between Protestants and Catholics (the Belgians are basically Dutch people who remained Catholic). If the Afghans are known as opium producers, the Belgians are known for producing another, more benign, stuff of sinful pleasures (chocolate). If the Taliban Afghans terrorize women, the Belgians are known for child pornography and abuse. Finally, if this image of the Belgians as chocolate-eaters and child-abusers is a media cliché, *so is the image of Afghanistan as a country of opium and female oppression*. It is like the old sad joke: 'Jews and cyclists are at the root of all our problems!' 'Why cyclists?' '*Why Jews?!*'

America's 'holiday from history' was a fake: America's peace was bought by the catastrophes going on elsewhere. These days, the predominant point of view is that of an innocent gaze confronting unspeakable Evil which struck from the Outside – and again, apropos of this gaze, we should summon up the strength to apply to it Hegel's well-known dictum that Evil resides (also) in the innocent gaze itself which perceives Evil all around. There is thus an element of truth even in the most constricted Moral Majority vision of a depraved America dedicated to mindless pleasures, in the conservative horror at this netherworld of sex-exploitation and pathological violence: what they don't get is merely the Hegelian speculative identity between this netherworld and their own position of fake purity – the fact that so many fundamentalist preachers have turned out to be secret sexual perverts is more than a contingent empirical fact. The infamous Jimmy Swaggart's claim that the fact that he visited prostitutes only gave additional strength to his preaching (he knew from intimate struggle what he was preaching against), although undoubtedly hypocritical on the immediate subjective level, is none the less objectively true.

Can we imagine a greater irony than the fact that the first codename for the US operation against terrorists was 'Infinite Justice' (later changed in response to the reproach from

American Islamic clerics that only God can exert infinite justice)? Taken seriously, this name is profoundly ambiguous: either it means that the Americans have the right ruthlessly to destroy not only all terrorists but also all who gave them material, moral, ideological, etc., support – and this process will be, by definition, endless in the precise sense of Hegelian 'bad infinity', the work will never really be accomplished, there will always be some other terrorist threat (and, in fact, in April 2002, Dick Cheney directly stated that the 'war on terrorism' will probably never end, at least not in our lifetimes); or it means that the justice exerted must be truly infinite in the strict Hegelian sense – that, in relating to others, it has to relate to itself: in short, that it has to ask how we ourselves, who exert justice are involved in what we are fighting against. When, on September 22 2001, Jacques Derrida received the Theodor Adorno award, he referred in his speech to the WTC attacks: 'My unconditional compassion, addressed at the victims of September 11, does not prevent me from saying aloud: with regard to this crime, I do not believe that anyone is politically guiltless.' This self-relating, this inclusion of oneself in the picture, is the only true 'infinite justice'.

Against the cynical double-talk about 'infinite justice', I am tempted to recall the words of the Taliban leader Mullah Mohammed Omar in his address to the American people on September 25 2001: 'You accept everything your government says, whether it is true or false . . . Can't you think for yourselves? . . . It would be better for you to use your own sense and understanding.' While these statements are undoubtedly a cynical manipulation (what about giving the same right to use one's own sense and understanding to Afghans themselves?), are they not nevertheless, when taken in an abstract decontextualized sense, quite appropriate?

3

HAPPINESS AFTER
SEPTEMBER 11

In psychoanalysis, the betrayal of desire has a precise name: happiness. When, exactly, can people be said to be happy? In a country like Czechoslovakia in the late 1970s and 1980s, people actually were in a way happy: three fundamental conditions of happiness were fulfilled there.

1. Their material needs were basically satisfied – not *too* well satisfied, since the excess of consumption can in itself generate unhappiness. It is good to experience a brief shortage of some goods on the market from time to time (no coffee for a couple of days, then no beef, then no TV sets): these brief periods of shortage functioned as exceptions which reminded people that they should be glad that such goods were generally available – if everything is available all the time, people take this availability as an evident fact of life, and no longer appreciate their luck. Thus life went on in a regular and predictable way, without any great efforts or shocks; one was allowed to withdraw into one's own private world.

2. A second – extremely important – feature: there was the

Other (the Party) to be blamed for everything that went wrong, so that one did not feel truly responsible – if there was a temporary shortage of some goods, even if a storm caused great damage, it was 'their' fault.

3. And – last, but not least – there was an Other Place (the consumerist West) which one was allowed to dream about, and even visit sometimes – this place was just at the right distance: not too far away, not too near.

This fragile balance was disturbed – by what? By desire, precisely. Desire was the force which compelled the people to go further – and end up in a system in which the vast majority are definitely *less* happy.

Happiness is thus – to put it in Alain Badiou's terms – not a category of truth, but a category of mere Being, and, as such, confused, indeterminate, inconsistent (take the proverbial answer of a German immigrant to the USA who, asked: 'Are you happy?', answered: 'Yes, yes, I am very happy, *aber glücklich bin ich nicht . . .*'). It is a *pagan* concept: for pagans, the goal of life is to be happy (the idea of living 'happily ever after' is a Christianized version of paganism), and religious experience and political activity are considered the highest forms of happiness (see Aristotle) – no wonder the Dalai Lama has had such success recently preaching the gospel of happiness around the world, and no wonder he is finding the greatest response precisely in the USA, the ultimate empire of the (pursuit of) happiness. . . . In short, 'happiness' belongs to the pleasure principle, and what undermines it is the insistence of a Beyond of the pleasure principle.

In a strict Lacanian sense of the term, we should thus posit that 'happiness' relies on the subject's inability or unreadiness fully to confront the consequences of its desire: the price of happiness is that the subject remains stuck in the inconsistency of its desire. In our daily lives, we (pretend to) desire things which we do not really desire, so that, ultimately, the worst thing that can happen is for us to get what we 'officially' desire. Happiness is thus inherently hypocritical: it is the happiness of dreaming about things we do not really want. When today's Left bombards the capitalist system with demands that it obviously cannot fulfil (Full employment! Retain the welfare state! Full rights for immigrants!), it is basically playing a game of hysterical provocation, of addressing the Master with a demand which will be impossible for him to meet, and will thus expose his impotence. The problem with this strategy, however, is not only that the system cannot meet these demands, but that, in addition, those who voice them do not really want them to be realized. For example, when 'radical' academics demand full rights for immigrants and opening of the borders, are they aware that the direct implementation of this demand would, for obvious reasons, inundate developed Western countries with millions of newcomers, thus provoking a violent working-class racist backlash which would then endanger the privileged position of these very academics? Of course they are, but they count on the fact that their demand will not be met – in this way, they can hypocritically retain their clear radical conscience while continuing to enjoy their privileged position. In 1994, when a new wave of emigration from Cuba to the USA was on the cards, Fidel Castro warned the USA that if they did not stop inciting Cubans to emigrate, Cuba would no longer prevent them from doing it – which the Cuban authorities in effect did a couple of days later, embarrassing the USA with thousands of unwanted newcomers. . . . Is this not like the proverbial woman who snapped back at a man who was making macho advances to her: 'Shut up, or you'll have to do what you're boasting about!'

In both cases, the gesture is that of calling the other's bluff, counting on the fact that what the other really fears is that one will fully comply with his or her demand. And would not the same gesture also throw our radical academics into a panic? Here the old '68 motto *'Soyons réalistes, demandons l'impossible!'* acquires a new cynical and sinister meaning which, perhaps, reveals its truth: 'Let's be realists: we, the academic Left, want to appear critical, while fully enjoying the privileges the system offers us. So let's bombard the system with impossible demands: we all know that these demands won't be met, so we can be sure that nothing will actually change, and we'll maintain our privileged status!' If someone accuses a big corporation of particular financial crimes, he or she is exposed to risks which can go right up to murder attempts; if he or she asks the same corporation to finance a research project into the link between global capitalism and the emergence of hybrid postcolonial identities, he or she stands a good chance of getting hundreds of thousands of dollars.

Conservatives are therefore fully justified in legitimizing their opposition to radical knowledge in terms of happiness: knowledge ultimately makes us unhappy. Contrary to the notion that curiosity is innate to humans – that there is deep within each of us a *Wissenstrieb*, a drive to know – Jacques Lacan claims that the spontaneous attitude of a human being is that of 'I don't want to know about it' – a fundamental resistance against knowing too much. Every true progress in knowledge has to be bought by a painful struggle against our spontaneous propensities – is not today's biogenetics the clearest proof of these limits of our readiness to know? The gene responsible for Huntington's chorea is isolated, so that each of us can learn precisely not only if he or she will get Huntington's, but also when he or she will get it. The onset of the disease depends on a genetic transcription error – the stuttering repetition of the 'word' CAG in the middle of the gene: the age at which the illness will appear depends strictly and implacably on the number of repetitions of CAG in one place in this gene (if there are forty repetitions, you will get the first symptoms at fifty-nine; if forty-one, at

fifty-four . . . if fifty, at twenty-seven). A good lifestyle, physical fitness, the best medicine, healthy food, family love and
support can do nothing about it – pure fatalism, undiluted by
environmental variability. There is as yet no cure; we can do
nothing about it.[25] So what should we do when we know that we
can submit ourselves to testing and thus acquire knowledge
which, if positive, tells us exactly when we will go mad and die?
Can we imagine a clearer confrontation with the meaningless
contingency that rules our life?

Thus Huntington's chorea presents us with a disturbing alternative: if there is a history of this disease in my family, should I
take the test which will tell me if (and when) I will inevitably get
it or not? What is the answer? If I cannot bear the prospect of
knowing when I will die, the (more fantasmatic than realistic)
ideal solution may seem to be the following one: I authorize
another person or institution whom I trust completely to test
me and *not to tell me the result*, only to kill me unexpectedly and
painlessly in my sleep just before the onslaught of the fatal illness, if the result was positive. . . . The problem with this
solution, however, is that *I know that the Other knows* (the truth
about my illness), and this ruins everything, exposing me to
horrifying gnawing suspicion.

Lacan drew attention to the paradoxical status of this *knowledge about the Other's knowledge.* Take the final reversal of Edith
Wharton's *Age of Innocence,* in which the husband, who for many
years has harboured an illicit passionate love for Countess
Olenska, learns that his young wife *knew* about his secret passion
all the time. Perhaps this would also offer a way to redeem the
unfortunate *Bridges of Madison County*: if, at the end for the film,
the dying Francesca were to learn that her allegedly simple-
minded, down-to-earth husband knew all the time about her

25 See Matt Ridley, *Genome*, New York: Perennial 2000, p. 64.

brief passionate affair with the *National Geographic* photographer, and how much this meant to her, but kept silent about it in order not to hurt her. That is the enigma of knowledge: how is it possible that the whole psychic economy of a situation changes radically not when the hero directly learns something (some long repressed secret), but when he *gets to know that the other* (whom he thought ignorant) *also knew it all the time,* and just pretended not to know in order to keep up appearances – is there anything more humiliating than the situation of a husband who, after a long secret love affair, learns all of a sudden that his wife knew about it all the time, but kept silent about it out of politeness or, even worse, out of love for him?

Is the ideal solution, then, the opposite one: if I suspect that my child may have the disease, I test him *without him knowing it*, and then kill him painlessly just before the onslaught? The ultimate fantasy of happiness here would be that of an anonymous state institution doing this for all of us without our knowledge – but, again, the question crops up: do we know about it (about the fact that the other knows) or not? The way to a perfect totalitarian society is open. . . . There is only one way out of this conundrum: what if what is false here is the underlying premise, the notion that the ultimate ethical duty is that of protecting the Other from pain, of keeping him or her in protective ignorance? So when Habermas advocates constraints on biogenetic manipulation with reference to the threat it poses to human autonomy, freedom and dignity,[26] he is philosophically 'cheating', concealing the true reason why his line of argument appears to be convincing: what he is really referring to is not autonomy and freedom, but happiness – it is on behalf of happiness that he, the great representative of the Enlightenment tradition, ended up

26 See Jürgen Habermas, *Die Zukunft der menschlichen Natur*, Frankfurt: Suhrkamp 2001.

on the same side as conservative advocates of blessed ignorance.

Which ideological constellation sustains this 'pursuit of happiness'? The well-known and highly successful animated series *The Land Before Time*, produced by Steven Spielberg, provides what is arguably the clearest articulation of the hegemonic liberal multiculturalist ideology. The same message is repeated again and again: we are all different – some of us are big, some are small; some know how to fight, others know how to flee – but we should learn to live with these differences, to perceive them as something which makes our lives richer (recall the echo of this attitude in the recent reports on how the al-Qaeda prisoners are treated at Guantanamo Bay: they are given food appropriate to their specific cultural and religious needs, allowed to pray . . .). From and on the outside, we appear different, but inside, we are all the same – frightened individuals at a loss in the world, needing the help of others. In one of the songs, the big bad dinosaurs sing about how those who are big can break all the rules, behave badly, squash those who are helpless and small:

> When you're big / You can push all / The little ones around
> / They're looking up / While you are looking down . . .
> Things are better when you're big . . . All the rules that
> grown-ups made / They don't apply to you.

The answer of the small oppressed ones in the following song is not to fight the big ones, but to understand that, behind their bullying exterior, they are no different from us – secretly afraid, with their share of problems:

> They have feelings just like we do / They have problems too.
> / We think because they're big / they don't, but they do.
> They're louder and they're stronger, / and they make a

bigger fuss, / but way down deep inside / I think they're
kids like us.

The obvious conclusion is therefore the praise of differences:

It takes all sorts / To make a world / Short and tall sorts /
Large and small sorts / To fill this pretty planet / with love
and laughter. / To make it great to live in / Tomorrow and
the day after. / It takes all types / without a doubt / dumb
and wise types / every size types / To do all the things /
That need to be done / To make our life fun.

No wonder, then, that the final message of the films is that of
pagan wisdom: life is an eternal cycle in which older generations
are replaced by new ones, in which everything that appears has
to disappear sooner or later. . . . The problem, of course, is:
how far do we go? It takes all sorts – does that mean nice and
brutal, poor and rich, victims and torturers? The reference to
the dinosaur kingdom is especially ambiguous here, with its
brutal character of animal species devouring each other – is this
also one of the things that 'need to be done to make our life
fun'? The very inner inconsistency of this vision of the prelap-
sarian 'land before time' thus bears witness to how the message
of collaboration-in-differences is ideology at its purest – why?
Because, precisely, any notion of a 'vertical' *antagonism* that cuts
through the social body is strictly censored, substituted by
and/or translated into the wholly different notion of 'horizontal' differences with which we have to learn to live, because
they complement each other. The underlying ontological vision
here is that of the irreducible plurality of particular constellations, each of them multiple and displaced in itself, which can
never be subsumed under any neutral universal container. The
moment we find ourselves on this level, Hollywood meets the

most radical postcolonial critique of ideological universality: the central problem is perceived as that of impossible universality. Instead of imposing our notion of universality (universal human rights, etc.), universality – the shared space of understanding between different cultures – should be conceived of as an infinite task of translation, a constant reworking of one's own particular position. Is it necessary to add that this notion of universality as the infinite work of translation has nothing whatsoever to do with those magic moments in which effective universality makes its violent appearance in the guise of a shattering ethico-political *act*? The actual universality is not the never-won neutral space of translation from one particular culture to another, but, rather, the violent experience of how, across the cultural divide, we share the same antagonism.

At this point, of course, an obvious cricitism imposes itself: is not such tolerant Hollywood wisdom a caricature of truly radical postcolonial studies? To this, we should reply: *is it really?* If anything, there is more truth in this simplified flat caricature than in the most elaborated postcolonial theory: at least Hollywood distils the actual ideological message out of the pseudo-sophisticated jargon. Today's hegemonic attitude is that of 'resistance' – all the poetics of the dispersed marginal sexual, ethnic, lifestyle 'multitudes' (gays, the mentally ill, prisoners . . .) 'resisting' the mysterious central (capitalized) Power. Everyone 'resists' – from gays and lesbians to Rightist survivalists – so why not draw the logical conclusion that this discourse of 'resistance' is the norm today, and, as such, the main obstacle to the emergence of the discourse which would actually question the dominant relations?[27] So the first thing to

27 Along these lines, we should especially emphasize the ambiguous ('undecidable', to use the fashionable term) nature of contemporary feminism in developed Western countries – the predominant American feminism, with its legalistic twist *à la* Catherine

do is to attack the very core of this hegemonic attitude, the notion that 'respect for Otherness' is the most elementary ethical axiom:

> I must particularly insist that the formula 'respect for the Other' has nothing to do with any serious definition of Good and Evil. What does 'respect for the Other' mean when one is at war against an enemy, when one is brutally left by a woman for someone else, when one must judge the works of a mediocre 'artist,' when science is faced with obscurantist sects, etc.? Very often, it is the 'respect for Others' that is injurious, that is Evil. Especially when it is resistance against others, or even hatred of others, that drives a subjectively just action.[28]

The obvious criticism here is: do not Badiou's own examples display the limit of his logic? Yes, hatred for the enemy, intolerance of false wisdom, and so on, but is not the lesson of the last century that even – and especially – when we are caught up in such a struggle, we should respect a certain limit – the limit, precisely, of the Other's radical Otherness? We should never reduce the Other to our enemy, to the bearer of false knowledge, and so forth: always in him or her there is the Absolute of the impenetrable abyss of another person. The twentieth century's totalitarianism, with its millions of victims, shows the ultimate outcome of following to the end what appears to us a

MacKinnon, is ultimately a profoundly reactionary ideological movement, always ready to legitimize US army interventions with feminist concerns, always there to make dismissive patronizing remarks about Third World populations (from its hypocritical obsession with clitoridectomy to MacKinnon's racist remarks about how ethnic cleansing and rape are in Serb genes . . .).

28 'On Evil: An Interview With Alain Badiou', *Cabinet*, Issue 5 (Winter 2001), p. 72.

'subjectively just action' – no wonder, then, that Badiou ended up directly supporting Communist terror.

This, precisely, is the line of reasoning we should reject; let us take the extreme case, a mortal and violent struggle against a Fascist enemy. Should we show respect for the abyss of the radical Otherness of Hitler's personality beneath all his evil acts? It is here that we should apply Christ's famous words about how he has come to bring the sword and division, not unity and peace: *out of our very love for humanity*, including (whatever remains of) the humanity of the Nazis themselves, we should fight them in an absolutely ruthless and disrespectful way. In short, the Jewish saying often quoted apropos of the Holocaust ('When somebody saves one man from death, he saves the whole of humanity') should be supplemented with: 'When somebody kills just one true enemy of humanity, he (not kills, but) *saves* the whole of humanity.' The true ethical test is not only the readiness to save victims, but also – even more, perhaps – the ruthless dedication to annihilating those who made them victims.

What the emphasis on multitude and diversity masks is, of course, the underlying monotony of today's global life. In his perspicuous booklet on Deleuze,[29] Alain Badiou drew attention to how, if ever there was a philosopher who, apropos of any topic whatsoever, from philosophy to literature and cinema, repeated and rediscovered the same conceptual matrix again and again, it was Deleuze. The irony of this insight is that this, precisely, is the standard criticism of Hegel – whatever he is writing or talking about, Hegel always manages to squeeze it into the same mould of the dialectical process. Is there not a kind of poetic justice in the fact that the one philosopher about

---

29 See Alain Badiou, *Deleuze*, Paris: Hachette 1997.

whom one can in fact make this claim is Deleuze, *the* anti-Hegelian? And this is especially pertinent with regard to social analysis: is there anything more monotonous than the Deleuzian poetry of contemporary life as the decentred proliferation of multitudes, of non-totalizable differences? What occludes (and thereby sustains) this monotony is the multiplicity of resignifications and displacements to which the basic ideological texture is submitted.

Unbreakable (M. Night Shyamalan, 2000 – with Bruce Willis) is paradigmatic of today's ideological constellation in its very contrast between form and content. Its content cannot fail to strike us as childishly ridiculous: the hero discovers that he is actually a real-life comic-strip hero who cannot be wounded, who is invincible . . . As for its form, it is a rather refined psychological drama shot in a slow melancholic mood: the suffering of the hero who finds it traumatically difficult to accept what he really is, his interpellation, his symbolic mandate.[30] This is well illustrated in the scene where his own son wants to shoot him, thus proving to him that he really is invincible: when the father resists, the son starts to cry, desperate that his father is not able to accept the truth about himself. Why does Willis resist being shot at? Is he simply afraid to die, *or is he, rather, afraid of getting firm proof that he is invincible*? And is this not the same dilemma as that of Kierkegaard's 'sickness unto death'? We are afraid to discover not that we are mortal but, rather, that we are *immortal*. Here, we should link Kierkegaard with Badiou: it is difficult, properly traumatic, for a human animal to accept that his or her

---

30 And the difficulty of assuming interpellation is a great topic of post-traditional Hollywood. Which is the unifying feature between two Martin Scorsese films, *The Last Temptation of Christ* and *Kundun*? In both cases, the human incarnation of the divine figure (Christ, the Dalai Lama) is depicted in the difficult process of assuming his mandate.

life is not just a stupid process of reproduction and pleasure-seeking, but that it is in the service of a Truth. And this is how ideology seems to work today, in our self-proclaimed postideo-logical universe: we perform our symbolic mandates without assuming them and 'taking them seriously': while a father func-tions as a father, he accompanies his function with a constant flow of ironic/reflexive comments on the stupidity of being a father, and so on.

The recent Dreamworks animated blockbuster *Shrek* (Andrew Adamson and Vicky Jenson, 2001) expresses this pre-dominant functioning of ideology perfectly: the standard fairytale storyline (the hero and his endearingly confused comic helper go to defeat the dragon and save the princess from its clutches) is clothed in jokingly Brechtian 'extraneations' (when the large crowd observes the wedding in the church, it is given instructions how to react, as in the faked spontaneity of a TV show: 'Laugh!', 'Respectful silence!'), politically correct twists (after the kiss between the two lovers, it is not the ugly ogre who turns into a beautiful prince, it is the beautiful princess who turns into a plump ordinary girl), ironic stabs at feminine vanity (while the sleeping princess awaits her saviour's kiss, she quickly arranges her hair so that she appears more beautiful), unex-pected reversals of bad into good characters (the evil dragon turns out to be a caring female who later helps the heroes), up to anachronistic references to modern mores and popular culture.

Instead of praising these displacements and reinscriptions too readily as potentially 'subversive' and elevating *Shrek* into yet another 'site of resistance', we should focus on the obvious fact that, through all these displacements, *the same old story is being told*. In short, the true function of these displacement and sub-versions is precisely to make the traditional story relevant to our 'postmodern' age – and thus to prevent us from replacing it with a new narrative. No wonder the finale of the film consists of an ironic version of 'I'm a Believer', the old Monkees' hit from the 1960s: this is how we are believers today – we make fun of our beliefs, while continuing to practise them, that is, to rely on them as the underlying structure of our daily practices.

In the good old German Democratic Republic, it was impossible for the same person to combine three features: conviction (belief in the official ideology), intelligence, and honesty. If you believed and were intelligent, you were not honest; if you were intelligent and honest, you were not a believer; if you were a believer and honest, you were not intelligent. Does not the same also hold for the ideology of liberal democracy? If you (pretend to) take the hegemonic liberal ideology seriously, you cannot be both intelligent and honest: you are either stupid or a corrupted cynic. So, if I may indulge in a rather tasteless allusion to Agamben's *Homo sacer*, I can risk the claim that the predominant liberal mode of subjectivity today is *Homo sucker*: while he tries to exploit and manipulate others, he ends up being the ultimate sucker himself. When we think we are making fun of the ruling ideology, we are merely strengthening its hold over us.[31]

---

31 And this stance is far from being limited to Western 'postmodern' countries. In 2001, there emerged in Russia a movement called 'Walking Together', the official Putin youth organization whose ideology is 'Eurasian', advocating 'Russian values' against the West. One of their original ideas is to resort to burning books: in order to fight the influence of Western liberal decadence, they propose mass gatherings where people bring their decadent books and in return get free copies of proper Russian books, while the decadent books are thrown on a pile and publicly burned. Of course, this call to burning books was dismissed, in Russia itself and abroad, as a comic interlude not taken seriously by the top Putin nomenklatura itself; precisely as such, however, it works as an indication of a potential future – it was Herbert Marcuse who, apropos of Marx's *Eighteenth Brumaire*, claimed that, in the history of the emergence of Fascism, comedy *precedes* tragedy, the ultimate horror first appears as (is perceived as) operetta-like comedy.

There are two lessons to be drawn from this ideological constellation. First, we should be careful not to attribute to the Other the naive belief we are unable to sustain, transforming him or her into a 'subject supposed to believe', Even a case of the greatest certainty – the notorious case of the 'Muslim fundamentalist' on a suicide mission – is not as conclusive as it may appear: is it really so clear that these people, at least, *must* 'really believe' that, after their death, they will wake up in heaven with seventy virgins at their disposal (recall the story of a suicide terrorist who, before going to accomplish his mission, even sprinkled himself with perfume, so that he would smell nice for the virgins)? What if, however, they are terribly unsure about their belief, and they use their suicidal act as a means of resolving this deadlock of doubt by asserting this belief: 'I don't know if I really believe – but, by killing myself for the Cause, I will proof *in actu* that I believe . . .'? Similarly, we should avoid the conclusion that Aleksandr Fadeyev, the arch-Stalinist writer and president of the Soviet Writers' Union who shot himself after hearing Khrushchev's secret report at the Twentieth Congress, must have been an 'honest believer': in all probability, he was fully aware of the utter corruption of the system; what he believed in was the big Other, that is, the public appearance of the socialist New Man, and so on. Consequently, he did not kill himself because he learnt anything new in Khrushchev's report; none of his illusions was shattered – what was shattered was *his belief in the 'performative force' of the ideological illusion itself*.

Fadeyev's suicide may be compared to that of the German mayor who, in early 1945, when the US Army occupied his town and forced him to visit the nearby concentration camp, immediately committed suicide upon his return home: not because he was not aware of what was going on in the name of the regime he served, so that when he was confronted with the truth, he could not bear it, and killed himself; on the contrary, he knew more or less everything – the one who did not know was the big Other, the order of social appearances, so that his suicide was the ultimate act of hypocrisy, of *pretending* that he did not know. He killed himself to save the appearance of his honest ignorance. (It is almost as if Stalin was right when he condemned suicide as the act of ultimate cowardice, as the ultimate betrayal of the Party – at least if we apply his words to these cases. . . .)

The same goes for the much-celebrated 'honest Nazi', the mayor of a small East German town, who, when the Russians were approaching in February 1945, put on his mayoral uniform and all his medals, and took a stroll along the main street, where the Russians shot him down – in contrast to many others, who quickly destroyed all traces of their Nazi past: is this gesture – of publicly proclaiming one's allegiance to Nazi Germany in the hour of its defeat – really so noble? What was there for the mayor to be proud of? As if he did not know in what kind of state he was living! Was his gesture not also, therefore, a desperate hypocritical attempt to bestow a kind of nobility on a life which was – even in the very best of cases – full of compromises with the worst criminals?

The second lesson: instead of conceding any territory to the enemy in advance, we should struggle even for notions which appear to belong to the enemy 'naturally'. So, perhaps, we should unashamedly return to the great American tradition of Westerns, admired by Alain Badiou as the great genre of ethical *courage*. Of course, we cannot return to the naivety of the Westerns of the 1930s and early 1940s: the rise of what André Bazin called the 'meta-Westerns' of the early 1950s deprived the genre of its innocence. However, the genre was given a new lease of life in the second half of the 1950s – take Delmer Daves's two great masterpieces, *3.10 to Yuma* and *The Hanging Tree*, both far superior to the ultimate 'meta-Western' which seems to embody the courageous act at its purest, Fred Zinnemann's *High Noon*. What both films share is the structure of displaced decision: the key Act is performed not by the central character who appears to be the focus of the ethical ordeal, but by a secondary character who may even be the very source of temptation. (There is an echo of this even in *High Noon*: at the very end, it becomes clear that it is not Gary Cooper whose courage is in fact tested, but his young wife, played by Grace Kelly.)

3.10 to Yuma tells the story of a poor farmer (Van Heflin) who, for 200 dollars which he badly needs in order to save his cattle from drought, accepts the job of escorting a bandit with a high price on his head (Glenn Ford) from the hotel where he is being held to the train that will take him to prison in Yuma. What we have, of course, is a classic story of an ethical ordeal; throughout the film, it seems that the person who is submitted to the ordeal is the farmer himself, exposed as he is to temptations in the style of the (undeservedly) more famous *High Noon*: all those who promised to help him abandon him when they discover that the hotel is surrounded by a gang sworn to save their boss; the imprisoned bandit himself alternately threatens the farmer and tries to bribe him, and so on. The last scene, however, in retrospect, totally changes our perception of the film: near the train, which is already leaving the station, the bandit and the farmer find themselves face to face with the entire gang waiting for the right moment to shoot the farmer, and thus free their boss. At this tense moment, when the situation seems hopeless for the farmer, the bandit suddenly turns to him and says: 'Trust me! Let's jump on the wagon together!' In short, the one who has really suffered an ordeal is the bandit, the apparent agent of temptation: at the end, he is won over by the farmer's integrity and sacrifices his own freedom for him.

And, *mutatis mutandis*, does not the same hold for all of us today – for 'progressive' Western intellectuals who pass high judgements about how either workers in our societies or Third World crowds cravenly betrayed their revolutionary vocation and succumbed to nationalist or capitalist temptations? Take the repellent figure of the comfortable, well-paid English or French 'radical Leftist' condemning the Yugoslav masses for succumbing to the ethnic siren songs in the late 1980s: it was these 'radical Leftists' who were actually on trial, and who miserably failed the test in their misperception of the post-Yugoslav war. The same goes even more for the liberal multiculturalists who deplore the rise of New Right violence in Western societies: by adopting an arrogant patronizing attitude towards the phenomena they condemn, they fail the test. . . . Yes, the reborn patriots are right: today we really need new courage, and it is the lack of this courage (which is ultimately always also the courage to question *one's own* position) which is most conspicuous in the reaction of American (and European) intellectuals to September 11 and its aftermath.

In the second part of *Harmonienlehre*, his major theoretical manifesto from 1911, Arnold Schoenberg develops his opposition to tonal music in terms which, superficially, almost recall late Nazi anti-Semitic tracts: tonal music has become a 'diseased', 'degenerated' world in need of a cleansing solution; the tonal system has succumbed to 'inbreeding and incest'; Romantic chords such as the diminished seventh are 'hermaphroditic', 'vagrant' and 'cosmopolitan' . . . nothing easier than to claim that such a Messianic-apocalyptic attitude is part of the same 'deeper spiritual situation' which gave birth to the Nazi 'final solution'. This, however, is precisely the conclusion we should avoid: what makes Nazism repulsive is not the rhetoric of a final solution as such, but the concrete twist it gives to it. Another popular topic of this kind of analysis is the allegedly 'proto-Fascist' character of mass choreography displaying disciplined movements of thousands of bodies (parades, mass performances in stadiums, etc.); if we also see this in Socialism, we immediately draw the conclusion that there is a 'deeper solidarity' between the two 'totalitarianisms'. Such a procedure, the very prototype of ideological liberalism, misses the point: not only are such mass performances not inherently Fascist; they are not even 'neutral', waiting to be appropriated by Left or Right – it was Nazism which stole them and appropriated them from the workers' movement, their original site of birth.

It is here that we should oppose the standard historicist genealogy (the search for origins, influences, etc.) to the strict Nietzschean genealogy. Apropos of Nazism, the standard genealogy is exemplified by the search for the 'proto-Fascist' elements or kernel out of which Nazism grew (when, in Wagner's *Ring*, Hagen chases the Rhine gold; when the German Romantics aestheticized politics . . .); while the Nietzschean genealogy fully takes into account the rupture constitutive of a new historical event: none of the 'proto-Fascist' elements is Fascist *per se*, the only thing that makes them 'Fascist' is their specific articulation – or, to put it in Stephen Jay Gould's terms, all these elements are 'ex-apted' by Fascism. In other words, there is no 'Fascism *avant la lettre*', because *it is the letter itself (the nomination) which makes Fascism proper out of the bundle of elements*.

Along the same lines, we should radically reject the notion that discipline (from self-control to physical training) is a 'proto-Fascist' feature – the very predicate 'proto-Fascist' should be abandoned: it is the exemplary case of a pseudo-concept whose function is to block conceptual analysis: when we say that the organized spectacle of thousands of bodies (or, say, the admiration of sports which demand great effort and self-control like mountain climbing) is 'proto-Fascist', are we saying absolutely nothing, we are simply expressing a vague association which masks our ignorance. So when, decades ago, kung fu films were popular (Bruce Lee, etc.), was it not obvious that we were deal-ing with a genuine working-class ideology of youngsters whose only path to success was the disciplinary training of their only possession, their bodies? Spontaneity and the 'let it go' attitude of indulging in excessive freedoms belong to those who have the means to afford it – those who have nothing have only their dis-cipline. The 'bad' physical discipline, if there is one, is not collective training but, rather, jogging and body-building as part of the subjective economy of the realization of the Self's inner potentials – no wonder an obsession with one's body is an almost obligatory part of ex-Leftist radicals' passage into the 'maturity' of pragmatic politics: from Jane Fonda to Joschka Fischer, the 'latency period' between the two phases is marked by the focus on one's own body.

There is a well-known Israeli joke about Bill Clinton visiting Bibi Netanyahu: when Clinton sees a mysterious blue phone in Bibi's office, he asks Bibi what it is, and Bibi answers that it allows him to dial Him up there in the sky. Upon his return to the States, the envious Clinton demands that his secret service should provide him with such a phone – at any cost. They deliver it within two weeks, and it works, but the phone bill is exorbitant – two million dollars for a one-minute talk with Him up there. So Clinton furiously calls Bibi and complains: 'How can you afford such a phone, if even we, who support you financially, can't? Is this how you spend our money?' Bibi answers calmly: 'No, it's not that – you see, for us, Jews, that call counts as a local call!' Interestingly, in the Soviet version of the joke, God is replaced by Hell: when Nixon visits Brezhnev and sees a special phone, Brezhnev explains to him that this is a link to Hell; at the end of the joke, when Nixon complains about the price of the call, Brezhnev calmly answers: 'For us in the Soviet Union, the call to Hell counts as a local call.'

A postmodern liberal democrat's first, quasi-automatic,

reaction to this joke would be: this, precisely, is the source of
Evil today – people who think they have a direct line to God
(Truth, Justice, Democracy, or some other Absolute), and feel
justified in denouncing others, their opponents, as having a
direct line to Hell (Evil Empires or axes of Evil); against this
absolutization, we should modestly accept that all our positions
are relative, conditioned by contingent historical constellations,
so that no one has definitive Solutions, merely pragmatic temporary solutions. The falsity of this stance was denounced by
Chesterton: 'At any street corner we may meet a man who
utters the frantic and blasphemous statement that he may be
wrong. Every day one comes across somebody who says that of
course his view may not be the right one. Of course his view
must be the right one, or it is not his view.'[32] Is the same falsity
not clearly discernible in the rhetoric of many a postmodern
deconstructionist? Chesterton is quite right to use the strong
term 'blasphemous', which must be given its whole weight
here: the apparently modest relativization of one's own position
is the mode of appearance of its very opposite, of privileging
one's own position of enunciation. Compare the struggle and
pain of the 'fundamentalist' with the serene peace of the liberal
democrat who, from his safe subjective position, ironically dis-
misses every full-fledged engagement, every 'dogmatic' taking
sides.

So are we preaching the old lesson of how the ideological
meaning of an element does not dwell in this element itself, but
hinges on the way it is 'appropriated', articulated into a chain?
Yes – with one fateful proviso: that we should summon up the
courage to abandon 'democracy' as the Master-Signifier of this
chain. Democracy is today's main political fetish, the disavowal

32 Chesterton, *Orthodoxy*, p. 37.

of basic social antagonisms: in the electoral situation, the social hierarchy is momentarily suspended, the social body is reduced to a pure multitude which can be numbered, and here the antagonism is also suspended. A decade ago, in the State of Louisiana's governor elections, when the only alternative to the ex-KKK David Duke was a corrupt Democrat, many cars displayed a sticker: 'Vote for a crook – it's important!' In the May 2002 French presidential elections, Front National leader Jean-Marie le Pen got through to the final round against the incumbent, Jacques Chirac, who is suspected of financial impropriety. Faced with this unenviable choice, demonstrators displayed a banner reading 'L'arnaque plutôt que la haine [Swindling is better than hating]'. That is the ultimate paradox of democracy: within the existing political order, every campaign against corruption ends up being co-opted by the populist extreme Right. In Italy, the ultimate outcome of the 'clean hands' campaign which destroyed the old political establishment centred on Christian Democracy is Berlusconi in power; in Austria, Haider legitimized his rise to power in anti-corruption terms; even in the USA, it is accepted common wisdom that Democratic Congressmen are more corrupt than Republican ones. The idea of a 'honest democracy' is an illusion, as is the notion of the order of Law without its obscene superego supplement: what looks like a contingent distortion of the democratic project is inscribed into its very notion – that is, democracy *is démocrassouille*. The democratic political order is of its very nature susceptible to corruption. The ultimate choice is: do we accept and endorse this corruption in a spirit of realistic resigned wisdom, or can we summon up the courage to formulate a Leftist alternative to democracy in order to break the vicious cycle of democratic corruption and the Rightist campaigns to get rid of it?[33]

33 This inherent limitation of democracy also accounts for the unique

Where, then, should we look for an alternative? Here, we should proceed with extreme caution and, simultaneously, without any prejudices – why should we not see emancipatory potential even in such an apparently 'reactionary' notion as 'Russian identity'? Perhaps the peculiarity of words can be our guide in this matter: often, in Russian, there are two words for (what appears to us, Westerners) the same term – one designating its ordinary meaning, the other a more ethically charged 'absolute' use. There is *istina*, the common notion of truth as adequacy to facts; and (usually capitalized) *Pravda*, the absolute Truth also designating the ethically committed ideal Order of the Good. There is *svoboda*, the ordinary freedom to do as we like within the existing social order; and *volja*, the more metaphysically charged absolute drive to follow one's will right up to self-destruction – as the Russians like to say, in the West, you have *svoboda*, but we have *volja*. There is *gosudarstvo*, the state in its ordinary administrative aspects; and *derzhava*, the State as the unique agency of absolute Power. (Applying the well-known Benjamin–Schmitt distinction, I may venture to claim that the difference between *gosudarstvo* and *derzhava* is the one between constituted and constituting power: *gosudarstvo* is the state administrative machine running its course prescribed by legal regulations; while *derzhava* is the agent of unconditional Power.) There are

power of fascination exerted by the figure of Salvador Allende: in so far as he tried to combine socialism with 'pluralist democracy', his true role is not that of a model to follow, but (independently of his subjective intentions) that of a negative hero whose task was to demonstrate, by means of his very defeat (tragic death in 1973), the impossibility of socialism without violence, in a 'soft' parliamentary way. That is to say, let us face it: we (old enough to be his contemporaries) all knew that his project was doomed, so that we were ultimately just waiting for it to happen, secretly even craving for his death.

intellectuals, educated people, and *intelligentsia*, intellectuals charged with and dedicated to a special mission to reform society.[34] (Along the same lines, there is already in Marx the implicit distinction between 'working class' – a simple category of social Being – and 'proletariat' – a category of Truth, the revolutionary Subject proper.)

Is not this opposition ultimately the one, elaborated by Alain Badiou, between Event and the positivity of mere Being? *'Istina'* is the mere factual truth (correspondence, adequacy), while *'Pravda'* designates the self-relating Event of truth; *'svoboda'* is the ordinary freedom of choice, while *'volja'* is the resolute Event of freedom. . . . In Russian, this gap is directly inscribed, appears as such, and thus reveals the radical risk involved in every Truth-Event: there is no ontological guarantee that *'Pravda'* will succeed in asserting itself at the level of facts (covered by *'istina'*). And, again, it seems as if the awareness of this gap itself is inscribed in Russian language, in the unique expression *awos* or *na awos*, which means something like 'on our luck'; it articulates the hope that things will turn out all right when one makes a risky radical gesture without being able to discern all its possible consequences – something like Napoleon's *on attaque, et puis on verra*, often quoted by Lenin. The interesting feature of this expression is that it combines voluntarism, an active attitude of taking risks, with a more fundamental fatalism: one acts, makes a leap, and then one hopes that things will turn out all right. . . . What if this stance is precisely what we need today, split as we are between

---

34 These distinctions are counterbalanced by some important condensations, multiple meanings of terms; say, the Russian term for peace, *mir*, also means 'world, universe' and the closed universe of the premodern farming village community, with the underlying idea, of course, that the whole cosmos is a harmonious Whole, like a well-regulated farming village.

Western utilitarian pragmatism and Oriental fatalism as the two faces of today's global 'spontaneous ideology'?

The Dutch Rightist populist politician Pim Fortuyn, killed in early May 2002, two weeks before elections in which he was expected to win a fifth of the votes, was a paradoxical symptomal figure: a Rightist populist whose personal features, and even (most of his) opinions, were almost perfectly politically correct: he was gay, had good personal relations with many immigrants, with an innate sense of irony, and so on – in short, he was a good tolerant liberal with regard to everything except his basic political stance. What he embodied was thus the intersection between Rightist populism and liberal political correctness – perhaps he had to die because he was living proof that the opposition between Rightist populism and liberal tolerance is a false one, that we are dealing with two sides of the same coin. Should we not, therefore, be striving for the exact opposite of the unfortunate Fortuyn: not the Fascist with a human face, but the freedom fighter with an inhuman face?

4

FROM *HOMO SUCKER* TO *HOMO SACER*

The danger the West is courting in its 'war on terrorism' was, yet again, clearly perceived by Chesterton who, in the very last pages of his *Orthodoxy*, that ultimate piece of Catholic propaganda, deployed the fundamental deadlock of pseudo-revolutionary critics of religion: they start by denouncing religion as the force of oppression which threatens human freedom; in fighting religion, however, they are compelled to forsake freedom itself, thus sacrificing precisely that which they wanted to defend – the ultimate victim of the atheist theoretical and practical rejection of religion is not religion (which, unperturbed, continues its life), but freedom itself, allegedly threatened by it. The radical atheist universe, deprived of religious reference, is the grey universe of egalitarian terror and tyranny:

> Men who begin to fight the Church for the sake of freedom and humanity end by flinging away freedom and humanity if only they may fight the Church . . . I know a man who has such a passion for proving that he will have no personal existence after death that he falls back on the position that he has

no personal existence now . . . I have known people who
showed that there could be no divine judgement by showing
that there can be no human judgement . . . We do not
admire, we hardly excuse, the fanatic who wrecks this world
for love of the other. But what are we to say of the fanatic
who wrecks this world out of hatred for the other? He sacrifices the very existence of humanity to the non-existence
of God. He offers his victims not to the altar, but merely to
assert the idleness of the altar and the emptiness of the
throne . . . With their oriental doubts about personality
they do not make certain that we shall have no personal life
hereafter; they only make certain that we shall not have a
very jolly or complete one here . . . The secularists have not
wrecked divine things; but the secularists have wrecked secular things, if that is any comfort to them.[35]

The first thing to be added to this today is that the same holds for
advocates of religion themselves: how many fanatical defenders
of religion started with ferociously attacking contemporary secular culture, and ended up forsaking religion itself (losing any
meaningful religious experience)? And is it not true that, in a
strictly homologous way, the liberal warriors are so eager to
fight antidemocratic fundamentalism that they will end up dis-
carding freedom and democracy themselves, if only they can
fight terrorism? They have such a passion for proving that non-
Christian fundamentalism is the main threat to freedom that
they are ready to fall back on the position that we have to limit
our own freedom here and now, in our allegedly Christian societies. If the 'terrorists' are ready to wreck this world for love of
the other, our warriors on terrorism are ready to wreck their
own democratic world out of hatred for the Muslim other. Alter

35 Chesterton, *Orthodoxy*, pp. 146–7.

and Dershowitz love human dignity so much that they are ready to legalize torture – the ultimate degradation of human dignity – to defend it.

Does the same not apply to the postmodern disdain for great ideological Causes – to the notion that, in our postideological era, instead of trying to change the world, we should reinvent ourselves, our whole universe, by engaging ourselves in new forms of (sexual, spiritual, aesthetic . . .) subjective practices? As Hanif Kureishi put it in an interview about his book *Intimacy*: 'Twenty years ago it was political to try to make a revolution and change society, while now politics comes down to two bodies in a basement making love who can re-create the whole world.' Confronted with statements like this, we can only recall the old lesson of Critical Theory: when we try to preserve the authentic intimate sphere of privacy against the onslaught of instrumental/objectivized 'alienated' public exchange, it is privacy itself which becomes a totally objectivized 'commodified' sphere. Withdrawal into privacy today means adopting formulas of private authenticity propagated by the recent culture industry – from taking lessons in spiritual enlightenment, and following the latest cultural and other fashions, to engaging in jogging and body-building. The ultimate truth of withdrawal into privacy is a public confession of intimate secrets on a TV show – against this kind of privacy, we should emphasize that, today, the only way of breaking out of the constraints of 'alienated' commodification is to invent a new collectivity. Today, more than ever, the lesson of Marguerite Duras's novels is relevant: the way – the *only* way – to have an intense and fulfilling personal (sexual) relationship is not for the couple to look into each other's eyes, forgetting about the world around them, but, while holding hands, to look together outside, at a third point (the Cause for which both are fighting, in which both are engaged).

The ultimate result of global subjectivization is not that 'objective reality' disappears, but that our subjectivity itself disappears, turns into a trifling whim, while social reality continues its course. Here I am tempted to paraphrase the interrogator's famous answer to Winston Smith, who doubts the existence of Big Brother ('It is You who doesn't exist!'): the proper reply to postmodern doubts about the existence of the ideological big Other is that it is the subject itself who doesn't exist. . . . No wonder that our era – whose basic stance is best encapsulated by the title of Phillip McGraw's recent bestseller, *Self Matters*, teaching us how to 'create your life from the inside out' – finds its logical supplement in books with titles like *How to Disappear Completely*: manuals about how to erase all traces of one's previous existence, and 'reinvent' oneself completely.[36] This is where we find the difference between Zen proper and its Western version: the true greatness of Zen is that it cannot be reduced to an 'inner journey' into one's 'true Self'; the aim of Zen meditation is, on the contrary, a total voiding of the Self, the acceptance that there is no Self, no 'inner truth' to be discovered. This is why the authentic Zen masters are fully justified in interpreting the basic Zen message (liberation lies in losing one's Self, in immediately uniting with the primordial Void) as identical to utter military fidelity, to immediately following orders and performing one's duty without consideration for the Self and its interests – that is, in asserting that the standard antimilitaristic

36 See Doug Richmond, *How to Disappear Completely and Never be Found*, Secausus: A Citadel Press Book 1999. This book belongs to a series of how-to manuals which, in effect, constitute a refreshingly obscene double of 'official' manuals like those of Dale Carnegie: books which directly address our publicly unacceptable desires – other titles in the series are: *Cheaters Always Prosper*; *Advanced Backstabbing and Mudslinging Techniques*; *Revenge Tactics*; *Spying on Your Spouse*, and so on.

cliché about soldiers being drilled to attain the stain of mindless subordination and carry out orders like blind puppets, is identical to Zen Enlightenment. This is how Ishihara Shummyo made this point in almost Althusserian terms of an act of interpellation which grasps the subject directly, bypassing hysterical doubt or questioning:

> Zen is very particular about the need not to stop one's mind. As soon as flintstone is struck, a spark bursts forth. There is not even the most momentary lapse of time between these two events. If ordered to face right, one simply faces right as quickly as a flash of lightning . . . If one's name were called, for example, 'Uemon,' one should simply answer 'Yes,' and not stop to consider the reason why one's name was called . . . I believe that if one is called upon to die, one should not be the least bit agitated.[37]

Far from denouncing this stance as a monstrous perversion, we should perceive in it an indication of how authentic Zen differs from its Western appropriation which reinscribes it into the matrix of 'discovery of one's true Self'. The logic of an 'inner journey', brought to the end, confronts us with the void of subjectivity and thus compels the subject to assume his or her full desubjectivization; the paradoxical Pascalian conclusion of this radical version of Zen is that, since there is no inner substance to religion, the essence of faith is proper decorum, obedience to the ritual as such. What Western Buddhism is not ready to accept is thus that the ultimate victim of the 'journey into one's Self' is this Self itself.

More generally, is this not the same lesson as Adorno's and

37 Quoted from Brian A. Victoria, *Zen at War*, New York: Weatherhilt 1998, p. 103.

Horkheimer's *Dialectic of Enlightenment*? The ultimate victims of positivism are not confused metaphysical notions, but facts themselves; the radical pursuit of secularization, the turn towards our worldly life, transforms this life itself into an 'abstract' anaemic process – and nowhere is this paradoxical reversal more evident than in the work of de Sade, where the unconstrained assertion of sexuality deprived of the last vestiges of spiritual transcendence turns sexuality itself into a mechanical exercise devoid of authentic sensual passion. And is not a similar reversal clearly discernible in the deadlock of today's Last Men, 'postmodern' individuals who reject all 'higher' goals as terrorist and dedicate their life to survival, to a life filled with more and more refined and artificially excited/aroused minor pleasures? In so far as 'death' and 'life' designate for Saint Paul two existential (subjective) positions, not 'objective' facts, we are fully justified in raising the same Paulinen question: Who is really alive today?[38]

What if we are 'really alive' only if we commit ourselves with an excessive intensity which puts us beyond 'mere life'? What if, when we focus on mere survival, even if it is qualified as 'having a good time', what we ultimately lose is life itself? What if the Palestinian suicide bomber on the point of blowing him- or herself (and others) up is, in an emphatic sense, 'more alive' than the American soldier engaged in a war in front of a computer screen against an enemy hundreds of miles away, or a New York yuppie jogging along the Hudson river in order to keep his body in shape? Or, in psychoanalytic terms, what if a hysteric is truly alive in his or her permanent excessive questioning of his or her existence, while an obsessional is the very model of choosing a 'life in death'? That is to say, is not the ultimate aim of his or her com-

---

38 I owe this point to Alain Badiou (intervention at the symposium *Paul and Modernity*, UCLA, 14–16 April 2002).

pulsive rituals to prevent the 'thing' from happening – this 'thing' being the excess of life itself? Is not the catastrophe he or she fears the fact that, finally, *something will really happen* to him or her? Or, in terms of the revolutionary process, what if the difference that separates Lenin's era from Stalinism is, again, the difference between life and death? There is an apparently marginal feature which makes this point clearly: the basic attitude of a Stalinist Communist is that of following the correct Party line against the 'Rightist' or 'Leftist' deviation – in short, steering a safe middle course; for authentic Leninism, in clear contrast, there is ulti-mately only one deviation, the Centrist one – that of 'playing it safe', of opportunistically avoiding the risk of clearly and exces-sively 'taking sides'. There was no 'deeper historical necessity' in the sudden shift of Soviet policy from 'War Communism' to the 'New Economic Policy' in 1921, for example – it was just a des-perate strategic zigzag between the Leftist and the Rightist line, or – as Lenin himself put it in 1922 – the Bolsheviks made 'all the possible mistakes'. This excessive 'taking sides', this permanent zigzagging imbalance, is ultimately (revolutionary political) life itself – for a Leninist, the ultimate name of the counterrevolu-tionary Right is the 'Centre' itself, the fear of introducing a radical imbalance into the social edifice.

It is thus a properly Nietzschean paradox that the greatest loser in this apparent assertion of Life against all transcendent Causes is actual life itself. What makes life 'worth living' is the very excess of life: the awareness that there is something for which one is ready to risk one's life (we may call this excess 'freedom', 'honour', 'dignity', 'autonomy', etc.). Only when we are ready to take this risk are we really alive. Chesterton makes this point apropos of the paradox of courage:

A soldier surrounded by enemies, if he is to cut his way out, needs to combine a strong desire for living with a strange carelessness about dying. He must not merely cling to life, for then he will be a coward, and will not escape. He must not merely wait for death, for then he will be a suicide, and will not escape. He must seek his life in a spirit of furious indifference to it; he must desire life like water and yet drink death like wine.[39]

The 'post-metaphysical' survivalist stance of the Last Men ends up in an anaemic spectacle of life dragging on as its own shadow. It is within this horizon that we should understand today's growing rejection of the death penalty: we should be able to discern the hidden 'biopolitics' which sustains this rejection. Those who assert the 'sacredness of life', defending it against the threat of transcendent powers which are parasitical upon it, end up in a 'supervised world in which we'll live painlessly, safely – and tediously',[40] a world in which, for the sake of its very official goal – a long and pleasurable life – all real pleasures are prohibited or strictly controlled (smoking, drugs, food . . .). Spielberg's *Saving Private Ryan* is the latest example of this survivalist attitude towards dying, with its 'demystifying' presentation of war as a meaningless slaughter which nothing can really justify – as such, it provides the best possible justification for Colin Powell's 'no-casualties-on-our-side' military doctrine. Here, we are not confusing the overtly racist Christian fundamentalist 'defence of the West' and the tolerant liberal version of the 'war on terrorism' which ultimately wants to save Muslims themselves from the fundamentalist threat: important as the difference between them is, they get caught up in the same self-destructive dialectics.

39 Chesterton, *Orthodoxy*, p. 9.
40 Christopher Hitchens, 'We Know Best', *Vanity Fair*, May 2001, p. 34.

And it is against the background of this underlying shift in 'biopolitics' that we should interpret a series of recent political statements which cannot fail to look like Freudian slips of the tongue. Asked by journalists about the goals of the American bombardment of Afghanistan, Donald Rumsfeld once simply answered: 'Well, to kill as many Taliban soldiers and al-Qaeda members as possible.' This statement is not as self-evident as it may appear: the normal goal of a military operation is to win the war, to compel the enemy to capitulate, and even the mass destruction is ultimately a means to this end. . . . The problem with Rumsfeld's blunt statement, as with other similar phenomena like the uncertain status of the Afghan prisoners at Guantanamo Bay, is that they seem to point directly to Agamben's distinction between the full citizen and *Homo sacer* who, although he or she is alive as a human being, is not part of the political community. This is the status of John Walker, the 'American Talib' – does he belong in an American prison or among the imprisoned Taliban? When they were designated by Donald Rumsfield as 'unlawful combatants' (in contrast to 'regular' prisoners of war), this does not simply mean that they are outlawed because of their criminal terrorist activity: when an American citizen commits a serious crime, like murder, he remains a 'lawful criminal'; the distinction between criminals and noncriminals does not overlap with the distinction between 'lawful' citizens and what in France are called *sans-papiers*. The excluded are not only terrorists, but also those who are on the receiving end of the humanitarian help (Rwandans, Bosnians, Afghans . . .): today's *Homo sacer* is the privileged object of humanitarian biopolitics: the one who is deprived of his or her full humanity being taken care of in a very patronizing way. We should therefore recognize the paradox that concentration camps and refugee camps for the delivery of humanitarian aid are two faces, 'human' and 'inhuman', of the same socio-logical formal matrix. In both cases, the cruel joke from Lubitch's *To Be or Not to Be* applies: asked about the German concentration camps in occupied Poland, 'Concentration Camp Erhardt' snaps back: 'We do the concentrating, and the Poles do the camping.'[41] In both cases, the population is reduced to an object of biopolitics. So it is not enough to enumerate examples of today's *Homo sacer*: the *sans papiers* in France; the inhabitants of the *favelas* in Brazil, people in African-American ghettos in the USA, and so on. It is absolutely crucial to supplement this list with the humanitarian side: perhaps those who are perceived as recipients of humanitarian aid are the figures of *Homo sacer* today.

The ultimate proof of this logic of *Homo sacer* occurred when, in the first days of March 2002, the remaining Taliban and al-Qaeda forces surprised the Americans and their allies with a ferocious defence, forcing them to retreat temporarily and even shooting down an American helicopter, thus violating the sacred principle of war without casualties. What was truly weird in the reports of these events in the American media was that they could conceal their surprise at the fact that the Taliban fought back, as if the ultimate proof that they are truly criminal terrorists ('unlawful combatants') is that, when they are fired on, they *shoot back*. . . . The same predicament is clearly discernible

41 And does not the same apply to the Enron bankruptcy in January 2002, which can be interpreted as a kind of ironic commentary on the notion of the risk society? Thousands of employees who lost their jobs and savings were certainly exposed to a risk, but without any true choice – the risk appeared to them like blind fate. On the contrary, those who did have inside information on the risks, as well as a chance to intervene into the situation (senior managers), minimized their risks by cashing in their stocks and options before the bankruptcy – thus actual risks and choices were nicely distributed. . . . So, again, apropos of the popular notion that today's society is that of risky choices, we can say that some (the Enron managers) do the choices, while others (the ordinary employees) do the risking. . . .

in reports from the occupied West Bank: when the Israeli Army, in what Israel itself describes as a war operation, attacks the Palestinian police force and systematically destroys the Palestinian infrastructure, their resistance is quoted as proof that we are dealing with terrorists. This paradox is inscribed into the very notion of the 'war on terrorism' – a strange war in which the enemy is criminalized if he simply defends himself and returns fire. A new entity is thus emerging which is neither the enemy soldier nor a common criminal: the al-Qaeda terrorists are not enemy soldiers, they are 'unlawful combatants'; but they are not simple criminals either – the USA was completely opposed to the notion that the WTC attacks should be treated as apolitical criminal acts. In short, what is emerging in the guise of the Terrorist on whom war is declared is precisely the figure of the political Enemy, foreclosed from the political space proper.

This is another facet of the new global order: we no longer have wars in the old sense of a regulated conflict between sovereign states in which certain rules apply (the treatment of prisoners, the prohibition of certain weapons, etc.). What remains are two types of conflict: either struggles between groups of *Homo sacer* – 'ethnic-religious conflicts' which violate the rules of universal human rights, do not count as wars proper, and call for 'humanitarian pacifist' intervention by Western powers – or direct attacks on the USA or other representatives of the new global order, in which case, again, we do not have wars proper, merely 'unlawful combatants' criminally resisting the forces of universal order. In this second case, we cannot even imagine a neutral humanitarian organization like the Red Cross mediating between the warring parties, organizing the exchange of prisoners, and so on: one side in the conflict (the US-dominated global force) already assumes the role of the Red Cross – it perceives itself not as one of the warring sides, but as a mediating agent of peace and global order crushing particular rebellions and, simultaneously, providing humanitarian aid to the 'local populations'. Perhaps, the ultimate image of the treatment of the 'local population' as *Homo sacer* is that of the American war plane flying above Afghanistan – one is never sure what it will drop, bombs or food parcels.

This weird 'coincidence of opposites' reached its peak when, in April 2002, Harald Nasvik, a right-wing member of the Norwegian parliament, proposed George W. Bush and Tony Blair as candidates for the Nobel Peace Prize, quoting their decisive role in the 'war on terror' as the greatest threat to peace today – the old Orwellian motto 'War is Peace' finally becomes reality. Perhaps the greatest irony of the situation is that the main 'collateral damage' for the West is the plight of the Afghan refugees and, more generally, the catastrophic food and health situation in Afghanistan; so that, sometimes, military action against the Taliban is almost presented as a means to guarantee the safe delivery of humanitarian aid. We thus no longer have the opposition between war and humanitarian aid: the two are closely connected; the same intervention can function on two levels simultaneously: the toppling of the Taliban regime is presented as part of a strategy to help the Afghan people oppressed by the Taliban – as Tony Blair said, perhaps we will have to bomb the Taliban in order to secure food transportation and distribution.[42]

42 Here we should analyse the opposition between the New World Order and its fundamentalist Enemy along the lines of Hegel's famous analysis of the opposition between Enlightenment and Faith in his *Phenomenology of Spirit*, where he demonstrates their hidden complicity, identity even – that is, how the two poles not only support each other, but even reproduce each other's structure. Today, the New World Order poses as the tolerant universe of differences, of coexistence of particular cultures; while the Enemy is depicted as the fanatical/intolerant exclusive One.

Are we, then, witnessing a rebirth of the old distinction between *human rights* and the *rights of a citizen*? Are there rights of all members of humankind (to be respected also in the case of *Homo sacer*), and the more narrow rights of citizens (those whose status is legally regulated)? What, however, if a more radical conclusion is to be drawn? What if the true problem is not the fragile status of the excluded but, rather, the fact that, on the most elementary level, we are *all* 'excluded' in the sense that our most elementary, 'zero' position is that of an object of biopolitics, and that possible political and citizenship rights are given to us as a secondary gesture, in accordance with biopolitical strategic considerations? What if this is the ultimate consequence of the notion of 'post-politics'? The problem with Agamben's deployment of the notion of *Homo sacer*, however, is that it is inscribed into the line of Adorno and Horkheimer's 'dialectics of Enlightenment', or Michel Foucault's disciplinary power and biopower: the topics of human rights, democracy, rule of law, and so on, are ultimately reduced to a deceptive mask for the disciplinary mechanisms of 'biopower' whose ultimate expression is the twentieth-century concentration camps. The underlying choice here seems to be the one between Adorno and Habermas: is the modern project of (political) freedom a false appearance whose 'truth' is embodied by subjects who lost the last shred of autonomy in their immersion into the late-capitalist 'administered world', or do 'totalitarian' phenomena merely bear witness to the fact that the political project of modernity remains unfinished? However, does this choice between a 'pessimistic' historico-political analysis pointing towards a final closure (today's society as the one in which the very gap between political life and mere life is disappearing, and the control and administration of 'mere life' is directly asserted as the essence

of politics itself), and a more 'optimistic' approach which perceives 'totalitarian' phenomena as a contingent 'deviation' of
the Enlightenment project, as the symptomal point at which
the 'truth' of the latter emerges, really cover the entire field?
What if they are two sides of the same coin, based on the
repression/exclusion of the same traumatic feature?

The 'totalitarian' notion of the 'administered world', in
which the very experience of subjective freedom is the form of
appearance of subjection to disciplinary mechanisms, is ultimately the obscene fantasmatic underside of the 'official' public
ideology (and practice) of individual autonomy and freedom: the
first has to accompany the second, supplementing it as its
obscene shadowy double, in a way which cannot fail to recall the
central image of the Wachowski Brothers' film *Matrix*: millions
of human *beings* leading a claustrophobic life in water-filled cra-
dles, kept alive in order to generate the energy (electricity) for
the Matrix. So when (some) people 'awaken' from their immersion in Matrix-controlled Virtual Reality, this awakening is not
an opening into the wide space of the external reality, but, in the
first moment, the horrible realization of this enclosure, where
each of us is effectively just a foetus-like organism, immersed in
the amniotic fluid.

This utter passivity is the foreclosed fantasy that sustains our
conscious experience as active, self-positing subjects – it is the
ultimate perverse fantasy: the notion that, in our innermost
being, we are instruments of the Other's (Matrix's) *jouissance*,
drained of our life-substance like batteries. That is the enigma of
this mechanism: why does the Matrix need human energy? The
purely energetic solution is, of course, meaningless: the Matrix
could easily have found another, more reliable source of energy
which would not have demanded the extremely complex
arrangement of Virtual Reality co-ordinated for millions of
human units. The only consistent answer is: the Matrix feeds on

human *jouissance* – here we are back at the fundamental Lacanian thesis that the big Other itself, far from being an anonymous machine, needs the constant influx of *jouissance*. This is how we should invert the state of things presented by *Matrix*: what the film presents as the scene of our awakening into our true situation is in fact its exact opposite, the very fundamental fantasy that sustains our being.

In 'Le prix du progrès', one of the fragments that conclude *The Dialectic of Enlightenment*, Adorno and Horkheimer quote the nineteenth-century French physiologist Pierre Flourens' arguments against medical anaesthesia with chloroform: Flourens claims that it can be proved that the anaesthetic works only on our memory's neuronal network. In short, while we are being butchered alive on the operating table, we fully feel the terrible pain, but later, when we wake up, we do not remember it. . . . For Adorno and Horkheimer, this, of course, is the perfect metaphor for the fate of Reason based on the repression of nature in itself: the body, the part of nature in the subject, fully feels the pain; it is just that, due to repression, the subject does not remember it. That is nature's perfect revenge for our domination over it: unknowingly, we are our own greatest victims, butchering ourselves alive. . . . Can we not also read this as the perfect fantasy scenario of interpassivity, of the Other Scene in which we pay the price for our active intervention in the world? There is no active free agent without this fantasmatic support, without this Other Scene in which he is totally manipulated by the Other. Perhaps the caricatural need of senior managers, daily deciding the fate of thousands of ordinary employees, to take refuge in playing the slave to a dominatrix in sado-masochistic spectacle has a deeper foundation than we may think.

Agamben's analysis should be given its full radical character of questioning the very notion of democracy; that is to say: his

SLAVOJ ŽIŽEK

notion of *Homo sacer* should not be watered down into an element of a radical-democratic project whose aim is to
renegotiate/redefine the limits of in- and exclusion, so that the
symbolic field will also be more and more open to the voices of
those who are excluded by the hegemonic configuration of the
public discourse. This is the gist of Judith Butler's reading of
Antigone: 'the limit for which she stands, a limit for which no
standing, no translatable representation is possible, is . . . the
trace of an alternate legality that haunts the conscious, public
sphere as its scandalous future.'[43] Antigone formulates her claim
on behalf of all those who, like the *sans-papiers* in today's France,
are without a full and definite socio-ontological status, and
Butler herself refers here to Agamben's *Homo Sacer*.[44] This is why
we should pin down neither the position from which (on behalf
of which) Antigone is speaking, nor the object of her claim:
despite her emphasis on the unique position of her brother, this
object is not as unambiguous as it may appear (is not Oedipus
himself also not her (half-)brother?); her position is not simply
feminine, because she enters the male domain of public affairs –
in addressing Creon, the head of state, she speaks like him,
appropriating his authority in a perverse/displaced way; neither
does she speak on behalf of kinship, as Hegel claimed, since her
very family stands for the ultimate (incestuous) corruption of
the proper order of kinship. Her claim thus displaces the fundamental contours of the Law, what the Law excludes and
includes.

Butler develops her reading in contrast to two main opponents – not only Hegel, but also Lacan. For Hegel, the conflict
is conceived as internal to the socio-symbolic order, as the tragic

43 Judith Butler, *Antigone's Claim*, New York: Columbia University
Press 2000, p. 40.
44 Ibid., p. 81.

split of the ethical substance: Creon and Antigone stand for its two components, state and family, Day and Night, the human legal order and the Divine subterranean order. Lacan, on the contrary, emphasizes how Antigone, far from standing for kinship, assumes the limit-position of the very instituting gesture of the symbolic order, of the impossible zero-level of symbolization, which is why she stands for the death drive: while she is still alive, she is already dead in terms of the symbolic order, excluded from the socio-symbolic co-ordinates. In what I am almost tempted to call a dialectical synthesis, Butler rejects both extremes (Hegel's location of the conflict within the socio-symbolic order; Lacan's notion of Antigone as standing for going-to-the-limit, for reaching the outside of this order): Antigone undermines the existing symbolic order not simply from its radical outside, but from a utopian standpoint of aiming at its radical rearticulation. Antigone is a 'living dead' not in the sense (which Butler attributes to Lacan) of entering the mysterious domain of Ate, of going to the limit of the Law; she is a 'living dead' in the sense of publicly assuming an uninhabitable position, a position for which there is no place in the public space – not a priori, but only with regard to the way this space is structured now, in historically contingent and specific conditions.

This, then, is Butler's central point against Lacan: Lacan's very radicality (the notion that Antigone locates herself in the suicidal outside of the symbolic order) reasserts this order, the order of established kinship relations, silently assuming that the ultimate alternative is the one between the symbolic Law of (fixed patriarchal) kinship relations and its suicidal ecstatic transgression. What about the third option: that of rearticulating these kinship relations themselves, that is, of reconsidering the symbolic Law as a set of contingent social arrangements open to change? Antigone speaks for all the subversive 'pathological' claims which crave to be admitted into the public space – to identify what she stands for in this reading with *Homo sacer,* however, misses the basic thrust of Agamben's analysis: there is no place in Agamben for the 'democratic' project of 'renegotiating' the limit which separates full citizens from *Homo sacer* by gradually allowing their voices to be heard; his point is, rather, that in today's 'post-politics,' the very democratic public space is a mask concealing the fact that, ultimately, we are all *Homo sacer.* Does this mean, then, that Agamben fully and simply shares the view of those who, like Adorno and Foucault, identify as the secret telos of the development of our societies a total closure of the 'administered world' in which we are all reduced to the status of objects of 'biopolitics'? Although Agamben denies that there is any 'democratic' way out, in his detailed reading of Saint Paul he violently reasserts the 'revolutionary' Messianic dimension – and if this Messianic dimension means anything at all, it means that 'mere life' is no longer the ultimate terrain of politics.[45] That is to say: what is suspended in the Messianic attitude of 'awaiting the end of time' is precisely the central place of 'mere life'; in clear contrast, the fundamental feature of post-politics is the reduction of politics to 'biopolitics' in the precise sense of administering and regulating 'mere life'.

This (mis)appropriation of Agamben is just one in the series of cases which exemplify a tendency of the American 'radical' academia (even more illustrative than Agamben here is the case of Foucault): the appropriated European intellectual topos, with its emphasis on the closure of every democratic emancipatory project, is reinscribed into the opposite topos of the gradual and partial widening of democratic space. The obverse of this apparent political radicalization is that radical political practice itself

45 See Giorgio Agamben, *Le temps qui reste*, Paris: Éditions Payot & Rivages 2000.

is conceived of as an unending process which can destabilize, displace, and so on, the power structure, without ever being able to undermine it effectively – the ultimate goal of radical politics is gradually to displace the limit of social exclusions, empowering the excluded agents (sexual and ethnic minorities) by creating marginal spaces in which they can articulate and question their identity. Radical politics thus becomes an endless mocking parody and provocation, a gradual process of reidentification in which there are no final victories and ultimate demarcations – and, again, it was Chesterton who formulated the ultimate critique of this stance in his appraisal of the guillotine:

> The guillotine has many sins, but to do it justice there is nothing evolutionary about it. The favourite evolutionary argument finds its best answer in the axe. The Evolutionist says, 'Where do you draw the line?' The Revolutionist answers, 'I draw it *here*: exactly between your head and body.' There must at any given moment be an abstract right or wrong if any blow is to be struck; there must be something eternal if there is to be anything sudden.[46]

It is on this basis that we can understand why Badiou, *the* theorist of the Act, has to refer to Eternity: an act is conceivable only as the intervention of Eternity into time. Historicist evolutionism leads to endless procrastination; the situation is always too complex; there are always more aspects to be accounted for; our weighing of the pros and cons is never over . . . against this stance, the passage to the act involves a gesture of radical and violent simplification, a cut like that of the proverbial Gordian

46 Chesterton, *Orthodoxy*, p. 116.

knot: the magical moment when the infinite pondering crystallizes itself into a simple 'yes' or 'no'.

If, then, against these misreadings, we resist the temptation to deprive the notion of *Homo sacer* of its true radicality, it allows us to analyse the numerous calls for rethinking some basic ingredients of modern notions of human dignity and freedom which abound after September 11. A good example is Jonathan Alter's *Newsweek* magazine column 'Time to Think about Torture', with the ominous subtitle 'It's a new world, and survival may well require old techniques that seemed out of the question'. After flirting with the Israeli idea of legitimizing physical and psychological torture in cases of extreme urgency (when we know that a terrorist prisoner possesses information which may save hundreds of lives), and 'neutral' statements like 'Some torture clearly works', Alter concludes:

> We can't legalize torture; it's contrary to American values. But even as we continue to speak out against human-rights abuses around the world, we need to keep an open mind about certain measures to fight terrorism, like court-sanctioned psychological interrogation. And we'll have to think about transferring some suspects to our less squeamish allies, even if that's hypocritical. Nobody said this was going to be pretty.[47]

The obscenity of such statements is blatant. First, why use the WTC attacks as justification? Are there not much more horrible crimes going on around the world all the time? Secondly, what is new about this idea? Did the CIA not teach the Latin American and Third World American military allies the practice of torture for decades? Hypocrisy has gone on for decades. . . . Even Alan Dershowitz's much-quoted 'liberal' argument is

47 *Newsweek*, 5 November 2001, p. 45.

suspicious: 'I'm not in favour of torture, but if you're going to have it, it should damn well have court approval.' The underlying logic – 'Since we are doing it in any case, better to legalize it, and thus prevent excesses!' – is extremely dangerous: it gives legitimacy to torture, and thus opens up the space for more illicit torture. When, along the same lines, Dershowitz argues that torture in the 'ticking clock' situation is not against the prisoner's rights as an accused person (the information obtained will not be used in a trial against him, and the torture is done not as punishment, only in order to prevent the mass killing to come), the underlying premise is even more disturbing: so one should be allowed to torture people not as part of a deserved punishment, but simply because they know something? Why, then, not also legalize the torture of prisoners of war who may possess information which may save hundreds of our soldiers' lives? Against liberal Dershowitz's honesty, we should therefore paradoxically stick to the apparent 'hypocrisy': OK, we can well imagine that in a specific situation, confronted with the proverbial 'prisoner who knows' and whose words can save thousands, we would resort to torture – even (or, rather, precisely) in such a case, however, it is absolutely crucial that we do *not* elevate this desperate choice into a universal principle; following the unavoidable brutal urgency of the moment, we should simply do it. Only in this way, in the very inability or prohibition to elevate what we had to do into a universal principle, do we retain the sense of guilt, the awareness of the inadmissibility of what we have done.

In short, such debates, such exhortations to 'keep an open mind', should be the sign for every authentic liberal that the terrorists are winning. And, in a way, essays like Alter's, which do not advocate torture outright, simply introduce it as a legitimate topic of debate, are even more dangerous than an explicit endorsement of torture: while – for the moment, at least – an explicit endorsement would be too shocking and therefore rejected, the mere introduction of torture as a legitimate topic allows us to entertain the idea while retaining a pure conscience ('Of course I'm against torture – whom does it hurt if we simply discuss it!'). Such legitimization of torture as a topic of debate changes the background of ideological presuppositions and options much more radically than its outright advocacy: it changes the entire field while, without this change, outright advocacy remains an idiosyncratic view. The problem here is that of fundamental ethical presuppositions: of course you can legitimize torture in terms of short-term gain (saving hundreds of lives) – but what about the long-term consequences for our symbolic universe? Where do we stop? Why not torture hardened criminals, a parent who kidnaps his child from a divorced spouse . . .? The idea that, once we let the genie out of the bottle, torture can be kept at a 'reasonable' level is the worst liberal illusion – if for no other reason than that the 'ticking clock' example is deceptive: for the most part, torture is not done in order to resolve a 'ticking-clock' situation, but for completely different reasons (to punish or break down the enemy psychologically, to terrorize the population to be subdued, and so on). Any consistent ethical stance must completely reject such pragmatic-utilitarian reasoning. Moreover, I am again tempted to conduct a simple mental experiment: let us imagine an *Arab* newspaper making the case for the torture of American prisoners – and the explosion of comments about fundamentalist barbarism and disrespect for human rights this would provoke! Of course, we should be fully aware of how our very sensitivity to torture – that is, the idea that torture is against the dignity of a human being as such – grew out of the ideology of modern capitalism itself: in short, the critique of capitalism is a result of capitalism's own ideological dynamics, not of our measuring it according to some external standard.

Far from being a single event, the topic of torture has persisted in 2002: at the beginning of April, when the Americans got hold of Abu Zubaydah, presumed to be the al-Qaeda second-in-command, the question 'Should he be tortured?' was openly discussed in the mass media. In a statement broadcast by NBC on 5 April, Donald Rumsfeld himself claimed that his priority is American lives, not the human rights of a high-ranking terrorist, and attacked journalists for displaying such concern for Zubaydah's well-being, thus openly clearing the way for torture; the saddest spectacle, however, was that of Alan Dershowitz who, in the guise of a liberal response to Rumsfeld, while accepting torture as a legitimate topic for discussion, in fact argued like the legalist opponents of the annihilation of the Jews at the Wannsee Conference. His reservations were based on two particular points: (1) the case of Zubaydah is not a clear case of the 'ticking-clock' situation – that is, it is not proven that he actually knows the details of a particular imminent mass terrorist attack which could be prevented by gaining access to his knowledge through torture; (2) torturing him would not yet be legal – in order to do such a thing, one should first engage in a public debate and then amend the US Constitution and publicly proclaim in what areas the USA will no longer abide by the Geneva Convention, which regulates the treatment of enemy prisoners . . . If ever there were an ultimate ethical fiasco of liberalism, this was it.

This reference to Wannsee is by no means a rhetorical exaggeration. If we are to believe the HBO docudrama about the Wannsee Conference, an old conservative lawyer there, shattered by the implications of the proposed measures (millions of Jews illegally liquidated), protested: 'But I visited the Führer a week ago, and he assured me solemnly that no Jew will suffer from illegal violent measures!' Reinhard Heydrich, who presided over the meeting, looked him in the eyes and, with a mocking smile, replied: 'And I am sure that if you ask him the same question again, he will give you the same reassurance!' The shattered judge got the point: that Nazi discourse operated on two levels; that the level of explicit statements was supplemented by an obscene unacknowledged underside. If we can rely on the surviving proceedings, then, throughout the conference, that was the central bone of contention between the hardline executives and 'legalists' like the judge who drafted the Nuremberg racial laws: while he passionately emphasized how much he hated the Jews, he nevertheless insisted that there were no proper legal grounds for the radical measures they were debating. The problem for the 'legalists' was thus not the nature of the measures, even less anti-Semitism as such, but their worry that such measures were not properly allowed in law – they were frightened to confront the abyss of a decision that was not covered by the big Other of the Law, by the legal fiction of legitimacy. Today, with the post-political regulation of the life of *Homo sacer*, this last reservation of the Nazi legalists has faded away: there is no longer any need to cover administrative measures with the legal big Other.

The unexpected precursor of this paralegal 'biopolitics' in which administrative measures are gradually replacing the rule of Law, was the Rightist authoritarian regime of Alfredo Stroessner in Paraguay in the 1960s and 1970s, which brought the logic of the state of exception to its unsurpassed absurd extreme. Under Stroessner, Paraguay was – in terms of its constitutional order – a 'normal' parliamentary democracy with all freedoms guaranteed; however, since, as Stroessner claimed, we all live in a state of emergency because of the worldwide struggle between freedom and Communism, the full implementation of the Constitution was forever postponed, and a permanent state of emergency was proclaimed. This state of emergency was suspended only for one day every four years, election day, so that free elections could be held, which legitimized the rule of Stroessner's Colorado Party with a majority of 90 per cent –

worthy of his Communist opponents . . . The paradox is that this state of emergency was the normal state, while 'normal' democratic freedom was the briefly enacted exception.

Did not this weird regime merely spell out in advance the most radical consequence of a tendency that is clearly perceptible in our liberal-democratic societies in the aftermath of September 11? Is not the rhetoric today that of a global emergency state in the fight against terrorism, which legitimizes more and more suspensions of legal and other rights? What is ominous in John Ashcroft's claim that 'terrorists use America's freedom as a weapon against us' is, of course, the obvious implicit conclusion: so, in order to defend 'us', we should limit our freedoms. . . . What the numerous highly problematic public statements by top American officials, especially Donald Rumsfeld and John Ashcroft, and also the explosive display of 'American patriotism' after September 11 (flags everywhere, etc.), indicate is precisely the logic of the state of emergency: the rule of law is potentially suspended; the State should be allowed to assert its sovereignty without 'excessive' legal constraints, since, as President Bush said immediately after September 11, America is in a state of war. The problem is that, precisely, America is obviously *not* in a state of war, at least not in the old conventional sense of the term (for the great majority of people, daily life goes on, and war remains the exclusive business of state agencies): the very distinction between the state of war and the state of peace is thus blurred; we are entering a time in which a state of peace itself can at the same time be a state of emergency.

Such paradoxes also provide the key to how the two logics of the state of emergency relate to each other: today's liberal-totalitarian emergency of the 'war on terrorism' and the authentic revolutionary state of emergency, first articulated by Saint Paul in what he called the emergency of the 'end of time'

approaching. The answer is clear: when a state institution proclaims a state of emergency, it does so by definition as part of a
desperate strategy to *avoid* the true emergency and return to the
'normal course of things'. There is one feature common to all
reactionary proclamations of a 'state of emergency': they have
all been directed against popular unrest ('confusion') and presented as a decision to restore normality. In Argentina, in Brazil,
in Greece, in Chile, in Turkey, the military proclaimed a state of
emergency in order to curb the 'chaos' of overall politicization:
'This madness must stop; people must return to their normal
jobs, work must go on!' In short, reactionary proclamations of
a state of emergency are a desperate defence against the true
state of emergency itself.

Along the same lines, we should be able to discern what is
really new in the list of seven states considered by the USA to be
the potential target of its nuclear weapons (not only Iraq, Iran
and North Korea, but also China and Russia): it is not the list as
such which is problematic, but its underlying principle –
namely, the abandonment of the golden rule of Cold War confrontation, according to which each of the superpowers publicly
proclaimed that under no conditions would it be the first to use
nuclear weapons: the use of nuclear weapons remained the
threat of MADness (Mutually Assured Destruction) which, paradoxically, guaranteed that no conflict would explode beyond
certain limits. The USA now renounced this pledge and proclaimed that it is ready to be the first to use nuclear weapons as
part of the war against terrorism, thus cancelling the gap
between ordinary and nuclear warfare, that is, presenting the
use of nuclear weapons as part of 'normal' war. I am almost
tempted to put it in Kantian philosophical terms: in the Cold
War, the status of nuclear weapons was 'transcendental', even
noumenal (they were not to be used in any actual war; rather,
they designated a limit of total destruction to be avoided in any

'empirical' warfare); while now, with the new Bush doctrine, the use of nuclear weapons is reduced to just another empirical ('pathological') element of warfare.

Another aspect of the same shift: in February 2002, a plan was announced – but quickly shelved – to establish an 'Office of Strategic Influence' among whose listed tasks was the dissemination of untruths in foreign media to propagate the image of the USA in the world. The problem with this office was not simply the open admission of lying; it was more along the lines of the well-known statement: 'If there is anything worse than a man lying, it is a man who is not strong enough to stand by his lies!' (This refers to the reaction of a woman to her lover, who wanted to have every form of sex except direct penetration, so that he would be able to avoid lying to his wife when he claimed that he was not having sexual intercourse with another woman – in short, he wanted to pull a Clinton on her. The woman was fully justified in claiming that in such circumstances, the outright lie – denial of extramarital sexual relations to his wife – would have been much more honest than his chosen strategy of lying in the guise of truth.) No wonder, then, that the plan was quickly shelved: a government agency announcing openly that its goal is, among others, to disseminate lies is self-defeating. What this means, of course, is that the official dissemination of lies will go on: the idea of a government agency directly dedicated to lying was, in a way, only too honest – it had to be shelved precisely in order to enable the efficient promulgation of lies.

The lesson to be learnt here – from Carl Schmitt – is that the divide friend/enemy is never just the representation of a factual difference: the enemy is by definition, always – up to a point, at least – *invisible*; he looks like one of us; he cannot be directly recognized – this is why the big problem and task of the political struggle is providing/constructing a recognizable *image* of the enemy. (This also shows why the Jews are the enemy *par excellence*:

it is not only that they conceal their true image or contours – it is that there is ultimately nothing beneath their deceptive appearance. Jews lack the 'inner form' that pertains to any proper national identity: they are a non-nation among nations; their national substance lies precisely in a lack of substance, in a formless infinite plasticity. . . .) In short, 'enemy recognition' is always a *performative* procedure which, in contrast to deceptive appearances, brings to light/constructs the enemy's 'true face'. Schmitt refers here to the Kantian category of *Einbildungskraft*, the transcendental power of imagination: in order to recognize the enemy, conceptual subsumption under pre-existing categories is not enough; one has to 'schematize' the logical figure of the Enemy, providing it with concrete tangible features which make it an appropriate target of hatred and struggle.

After 1990, and the collapse of the Communist states which provided the figure of the Cold War enemy, the Western power of imagination entered a decade of confusion and inefficiency, looking for suitable 'schematizations' for the figure of Enemy, sliding from narco-cartel bosses to a succession of warlords of so-called 'rogue states' (Saddam, Noriega, Aidid, Milošević . . .) without stabilizing itself in one central image; only with September 11 did this imagination regain its power by constructing the image of Osama Bin Laden, the Islamic fundamentalist *par excellence,* and al-Qaeda, his 'invisible' network. What this means, furthermore, is that our pluralistic and tolerant liberal democracies remain deeply 'Schmittian': they continue to rely on the political *Einbildungskraft* to provide them with the appropriate figure which reveals the invisible Enemy. Far from suspending the 'binary' logic Friend/Enemy, the fact that this Enemy is defined as the fundamentalist opponent of pluralistic tolerance simply adds a reflexive twist to it. Of course, the price of this 'renormalization' is that the figure of the Enemy undergoes a fundamental change: it is no longer the Evil

Empire, that is, another territorial entity (a state or group of states), but an illegal, secret – almost virtual – worldwide network in which lawlessness (criminality) coincides with 'fundamentalist' ethico-religious fanaticism – and since this entity has no positive legal status, this new configuration entails the end of the international law which – at least from the onset of modernity – regulated relations between the states.

When the Enemy serves as the 'quilting point' (the Lacanian *point de capiton*) of our ideological space, it is in order to unify the multitude of actual political opponents with whom we interact in our struggles. Thus Stalinism in the 1930s constructed the agency of Imperialist Monopoly Capital to prove that Fascists and Social Democrats ('Social Fascists') are 'twin brothers', the 'left and right hand of monopoly capital'. Thus Nazism itself constructed the 'plutocratic–Bolshevik plot' as the common agent who threatens the welfare of the German nation. *Capitonnage* is this operation by means of which we identify/ construct one sole agency which effectively 'pulls the strings' behind the multitude of actual opponents. And does not exactly the same hold for today's 'war on terrorism'? Is not the figure of the terrorist Enemy also a condensation of two opposed figures, the reactionary 'fundamentalist' and the Leftist protester? The title of Bruce Barcott's article in the *New York Times Magazine* on Sunday, April 7 2002 – 'The Color of Domestic Terrorism is Green' – says it all: not the Rightist fundamentalists responsible for the Oklahoma bombing and, in all probability, for the anthrax scare, but the Greens who did not kill any human being.

The truly ominous feature which underlies all these phenomena is this metaphorical universalization of the signifier 'terror': the message of the American TV campaign against drugs in spring 2002 was: 'When you buy drugs, you provide money for the terrorists!' – 'terror' is thus gradually elevated into the hidden universal equivalent of all social evils.

5

FROM *HOMO SACER* TO THE NEIGHBOUR

As Freud often emphasized, the key feature of dreams in which the dreamer appears naked in front of a crowd, the feature which provokes anxiety, is the weird fact that nobody seems to mind my nakedness: people simply walk by as if everything is normal. . . . Is this not like the nightmarish scene of the everyday racist violence which I witnessed in Berlin in 1992? At first, it seemed to me that, on the opposite side of the street, a German and a Vietnamese were simply playing some friendly game of performing an intricate dance around each other – it took me some time to grasp that I was witnessing an actual case of racial harassment: whichever way the perplexed and frightened Vietnamese turned, the German blocked his way, thus showing him that there was no place, no way to go, for him here, in Berlin. The cause of my initial misunderstanding was double: first, the fact that the German performed his harassment in a strange codified way, respecting certain limits, not going all the way through to physically attacking the Vietnamese; basically, he never actually touched him, he just blocked his path. The second cause, of course, was the fact that the people who were passing by (the event did take place on a busy street, not in a dark corner!) simply ignored – or, rather, *pretended* to ignore – the event, averting their eyes while hurrying along as if nothing special was going on. Is the difference between this 'soft' harassment and a brutal physical attack by a neo-Nazi skinhead all that remains of the difference between civilization and barbarism? Was not this 'soft' harassment, in a way, even worse? It precisely allowed the passers-by to ignore it and accept it as an ordinary event, which would not have been possible in the case of a direct brutal physical attack. And I am tempted to claim that a similar ignorance, a kind of ethical *epoche*, is mobilized when we are led to treat the other as *Homo sacer* – how, then, are we to break out of this predicament?

An epochal event took place in Israel in January and February 2002: the organized refusal of hundreds of reservists to serve in the occupied territories. These *refuseniks* (as they are referred to) are not simply 'pacifists': in their public proclamations, they emphasized that they did their duty in fighting for Israel in the wars against Arab states, where some of them were highly decorated. What they simply claim (and there is always something simple in an ethical act)[48] is that they cannot agree to fight 'in order to dominate, expel, starve and humiliate an entire people'. Their claims are documented by detailed descriptions of Israeli Defence Forces (IDF) atrocities, from the killing of children to the destruction of Palestinian property. This is how

48 The fine phrases which play a crucial historical role consist as a rule of tautological platitudes – from Rosa Luxemburg's 'freedom is freedom for those who think differently' up to Mikhail Gorbachev's famous warning to those who were not ready to follow his *perestroika*: 'One should not arrive too late, otherwise one will be punished by life.' Thus it was not the content of these phrases which counted, purely their structural role – if Luxemburg's statement had been made by a liberal critic of the Bolshevik revolution, it would have disappeared from memory long ago.

Gil Nemesh reports on the 'nightmare reality in the territories' on the protesters' website (seruv.org.il):

> My friends – forcing an elderly man to disgrace himself, hurting children, abusing people for fun, and later bragging about it, laughing about this terrible brutality. I am not sure I still want to call them my friends. They let themselves lose their humanity, not out of pure viciousness, but because dealing with it in any other way is too difficult.

A certain reality thus became perceptible: the reality of hundreds of small – and not so small – systematic daily humiliations to which the Palestinians are submitted – how Palestinians, and even Israeli Arabs (officially full citizens of Israel), are underprivileged in the allocation of water, in property deals, and so on. But more important than this is the systematic 'micro-politics' of psychological humiliations: the Palestinians are basically treated as evil children who have to be brought back to an honest life through stern discipline and punishment. Just consider the ridicule of the situation in which the Palestinian security forces are bombed, while at the same time pressure is put on them to crackdown on Hamas terrorists. How can they be expected to retain a minimum of authority in the eyes of the Palestinian population if they are humiliated daily by being attacked and, furthermore, by being expected simply to endure these attacks – if they defend themselves and fight back, they are again dismissed as terrorists? Towards the end of March 2002, this situation reached its ridiculous apogee: we had Arafat holed up and isolated in three rooms in his Ramallah compound, and at the same time asked to stop the terror, as if he has absolute power over the Palestinians. . . . In short, do we not find in the Israelis' treatment of the Palestinian Authority (attacking it militarily, while simultaneously, demanding that it should crack down on the terrorists in its own midst) a kind of pragmatic paradox in which the explicit message (the injunction to stop the terror) is subverted by the implicit message contained in the very mode of delivery of the explicit message? Is it not blatantly clear that the Palestinian Authority is thereby put into an untenable position: cracking down on its own people while being under fire from the Israelis? Is it not that the true implicit injunction is, rather, the opposite one: *we enjoin you to resist us, so that we can crush you?* In other words, what if the true aim of the present Israeli intrusion into Palestinian territory is not to prevent future terrorist attacks, but in fact to 'burn the bridges', to raise the hatred to a level which will prevent a peaceful solution in any foreseeable future?

The absurdity of the American view was perfectly expressed in a TV comment by Newt Gingrich on April 1 2002: 'Since Arafat is effectively the head of a terrorist organization, we will have to depose him and replace him with a new democratically elected leader who will be ready to make a deal with the State of Israel.' This is no empty paradox, but part of reality: Hamid Karzai in Afghanistan is already a 'democratic leader externally imposed on a people'. When Karzai, Afghanistan's 'interim leader' installed by the Americans in November 2001, appears in our media, he always wears the same clothes, which cannot fail to look like an attractive modernized version of traditional Afghan attire (a woollen cap and a pullover beneath a more modern coat, etc.) – his figure thus seems to exemplify his mission, that of combining modernization with the best of old Afghan traditions . . . no wonder, since this attire is the work of a top Western fashion designer! As such, Karzai is the best metaphor for the status of Afghanistan itself today. The real problem, of course, is: what if there simply is no 'truly democratic' (in the American sense of the term, of course) Palestinian silent majority? What if a 'new democratically elected leader' were to be even more anti-Israeli, since Israel does systematically apply the logic of collective responsibility and punishment, destroying the houses of the entire extended family of a suspected terrorist? The point is not the cruel arbitrary treatment as such, but, rather, that Palestinians in the occupied territories are reduced to the status of *Homo sacer*, the object of disciplinary measures and / or even humanitarian help, but not full citizens. And what the *refuseniks* accomplished is the passage from *Homo sacer* to 'neighbour': they treat the Palestinians not as 'equal full citizens' but as *neighbours* in the strict Judaeo-Christian sense.[49] And, in fact, that is the difficult ethical test for Israelis today: 'Love thy neighbour!' means 'Love the Palestinian!' (who is their neighbour *par excellence*), or it means nothing at all.

One cannot be enthusiastic enough about this refusal, which – significantly – was downplayed by the mass media: such a gesture of drawing the line, of refusing to participate, is an authentic *ethical act*. It is here, in such acts, that – as Saint Paul would have put it – there actually are no longer Jews or Palestinians, full members of the polity and *Homo sacer*. . . . We should be unashamedly Platonic here: this 'No!' designates the miraculous moment in which eternal Justice momentarily appears in the temporary sphere of empirical reality. The awareness of moments like this is the best antidote to the anti-Semitic temptation often clearly detectable among critics of Israeli pol-

---

49 Here we should note the difference between this Judaeo-Christian love for a neighbour and, say, the Buddhist compassion with suffering: this compassion does not refer to the 'neighbour' in the sense of the anxiety-provoking abyss of the Other's desire, but ultimately to the suffering which we, humans, share with animals (this is why, according to the doctrine of reincarnation, a human can be reborn as an animal).

itics. The fragility of the present global constellation is best expressed by simple mental experiments: if we were to learn of a threat to life on earth (say, that a gigantic asteroid will definitely hit the earth in eight months), how insignificant and ridiculous our most passionate ideologico-political struggles would look all of a sudden. . . . On the other hand, if (a more realistic expectation, perhaps) an unprecedented terrorist attack were to be accomplished (say, the nuclear destruction of New York and Washington, or millions poisoned by chemical weapons), how would this change our overall perception of the situation? The answer is not as simple as it may appear. However, what, even from the perspective of such a global catastrophe, would not appear ridiculous or insignificant are 'impossible' ethical acts. Especially now (spring 2002), when the cycle of violence between Israelis and Palestinians is progressively caught up in a self-propelling dynamic of its own, apparently impervious even to American intervention, it is only a miraculous *act* which can interrupt this cycle.

Our duty today is to keep track of such acts, of such ethical moments. The worst sin is to dissolve such acts in the false universality of 'no one is pure'. We can always play this game, which offers the player a double gain: that of retaining his moral superiority over those ('ultimately all the same') who are involved in the struggle, and that of being able to avoid the difficult task of committing himself, of analysing the constellation and taking sides in it. In recent years, it is as if the post-World War II anti-Fascist pact is slowly cracking: from historians-revisionists to New Right populists, taboos are tumbling down. . . . Paradoxically, those who undermine this pact refer to the very liberal universalized logic of victimization: certainly there were victims of Fascism, but what about other victims of the post-World War II expulsions? What about the Germans evicted from their homes in Czechoslovakia in 1945? Do not they too have some right to (financial) compensation?[50] This weird conjunction of money and victimization is one of the forms (perhaps even the 'truth') of money fetishism today: while many people reiterate that the Holocaust was the absolute crime, everyone speculates about appropriate *financial* compensation for it. . . . A key aspect of this revisionism is thus the relativization of guilt in World War II: the 'Did not the Allies also unnecessarily bombard Dresden?' type of argument. The latest most blatant example concerns the post-Yugoslav war. In Bosnia in the early 1990s, not all the actors were playing the same nationalist game – at some point, at least, the Sarajevo government – with its insistence that, against other ethnic factions, it stood for a multiethnic Bosnia and for the legacy of Tito's Yugoslavia – did take such an ethical stance against others fighting for their ethnic dominance. The truth of the situation was therefore not: 'Milošević, Tudjman, Izetbegovič, they're all the same in the long run' – such a generalization, which pronounces a universal dismissive judgement from its safe distance, is *the* form of ethical betrayal. It is sad to observe how even Tariq Ali, in his otherwise perspicacious analysis of the NATO intervention in Yugoslavia, falls into this trap:

> The claim that it is all Milošević's fault is one-sided and erro-
> neous, indulging those Slovenian, Croatian and Western
> politicians who allowed him to succeed. It could be argued,
> for instance, that it was Slovene egoism, throwing the
> Bosnians and Albanians, as well as non-nationalist Serbs and
> Croats, to the wolves, that was a decisive factor in triggering
> the whole disaster of disintegration.[51]

---

50 And does not the same apply to anti-abortion campaigns? Do not they also participate in the liberal logic of global victimization, extending it to the unborn?

51 Tariq Ali, 'Springtime for NATO', *New Left Review* 234 (March–April 1999), p. 70.

It is certainly true that other people's main responsibility for Milošević's success lay in their 'allowing him to succeed', in their readiness to accept him as a 'factor of stability', and tolerate his 'excesses' in the hope of striking a deal with him; and it is true that such a stance was clearly discernible among Slovene, Croat and Western politicians (for example, there are certainly grounds for suspecting that the relatively smooth path to Slovene independence involved a silent informal pact between the Slovene leadership and Milošević, whose project of a 'greater Serbia' had no need of Slovenia). However, two things must be added here. First, this argument itself implies that others' responsibility is of a fundamentally different nature from that of Milošević himself: the point is not that 'they were all equally guilty, participating in nationalist madness', but that others were guilty of not being hard enough on Milošević, of not opposing him unconditionally at any price. Secondly, what this argument overlooks is how the same reproach of 'egoism' can be applied to *all* the actors, including Muslims, the greatest victims of the (first phase of the) war: when Slovenia proclaimed independence, the Bosnian leadership openly supported the Yugoslav Army's intervention in Slovenia instead of risking confrontation at that early date, and thus contributed to their later tragic fate. So Muslim strategy in the first year of the conflict was also not without opportunism: its hidden reasoning was 'Let the Slovenes, Croats and Serbs bleed each other to exhaustion, so that in the aftermath of their conflict, we shall gain an independent Bosnia without paying a high price.' (It is one of the ironies of the Yugoslav–Croat war that two years earlier Colonel Arif Dudaković, the legendary Bosnian commander who successfully defended the besieged Bihać region against the Bosnian Serb army, commanded the Yugoslav Army units which were laying siege to the Croat coastal city of Zadar!)

There is a kind of poetic justice in the fact that the West

finally intervened apropos of Kosovo – let us not forget that it
was there that it all began, with Milošević's rise to power: this
rise was legitimized by the promise to remedy the underprivileged situation of Serbia within the Yugoslav federation,
especially with regard to Albanian 'separatism'. The Albanians
were Milošević's first target; afterwards, he vented his wrath on
other Yugoslav republics (Slovenia, Croatia, Bosnia), until,
finally, the focus of the conflict returned to Kosovo – as in a
closed loop of Destiny, the arrow returned to the one who dis-
patched it by freeing the spectre of ethnic passions. This is the
key point worth remembering: Yugoslavia did not start to
disintegrate when the Slovene 'secession' triggered the domino
effect (first Croatia, then Bosnia, then Macedonia . . .); it was at
the time of Milošević's constitutional reforms in 1987, depriv-
ing Kosovo and Vojvodina of their limited autonomy, that the
fragile balance on which Yugoslavia depended was irretrievably
disturbed. From that moment on, Yugoslavia continued to live
only because it had not yet noticed that it was already dead – like
the proverbial cat in the cartoon walking over a precipice, float-
ing in the air, and falling only when it becomes aware that it has
no ground beneath its feet. . . . From Milošević's seizure of
power in Serbia onwards, the only actual chance for Yugoslavia
to survive was to reinvent its formula: either Yugoslavia under
Serb domination, or some form of radical decentralization, from
a loose confederacy to the full sovereignty of its elements.

There is, however, a more crucial problem that we should
confront here: the uncanny detail that cannot fail to strike us in
the quote from Tariq Ali is the unexpected recourse, in the
midst of a political analysis, to a psychological category: 'Slovene
egoism' – why the need for this egregious reference? On what
grounds can one claim that Serbs, Muslims and Croats acted less
'egotistically' in the course of Yugoslavia's disintegration? The
underlying premise here is that when the Slovenes saw the

(Yugoslav) house falling apart, they 'egotistically' seized the opportunity and fled, instead of – what? Heroically throwing themselves, too, to the wolves? Thus the Slovenes are blamed for starting it all, for setting in motion the process of disintegration (by being the first to leave Yugoslavia) and, moreover, being allowed to escape without due punishment, suffering no serious damage. Hidden beneath this perception is a whole nest of classic Leftist prejudices and dogmas: the secret belief in the viability of Yugoslav self-management socialism, the notion that small nations like Slovenia (or Croatia) cannot in fact function like modern democracies, but, left to their own devices, necessarily regress to a proto-Fascist 'closed' community (in clear contrast to Serbia, whose potential to become a modern democratic state is never put in doubt).

This same nationalist bias is also discernible in the recent rise of anti-Americanism in Western Europe. No wonder this anti-Americanism is at its strongest in 'big' European nations, especially France and Germany: it is part of their resistance to globalization. We often hear the complaint that the recent trend of globalization threatens the sovereignty of the nation-state; here, however, we should qualify this statement: which states are most exposed to this threat? It is not the small states, but the second-rank (ex-)world powers, countries like the United Kingdom, Germany and France: what they fear is that once they are fully immersed in the newly emerging global Empire, they will be reduced to the same level as, say, Austria, Belgium, or even Luxembourg. The refusal of 'Americanization' in France, shared by many Leftists and Rightist nationalists, is thus ultimately the refusal to accept the fact that France itself is losing its hegemonic role in Europe. The levelling of weight between larger and smaller nation-states should thus be counted among the beneficial effects of globalization: beneath the contemptuous deriding of the new Eastern European post-Communist states, it is easy to discern the contours of the wounded narcissism of the European 'great nations'.

In 1990, Habermas also expressed his opinion that 'separatist' republics like Slovenia or Croatia do not possess enough democratic substance to survive as modern sovereign states. He thereby articulated a cliché: not only for the Serbs, but even for the majority of the Western powers, Serbia was self-evidently perceived as the only ethnic entity with enough substance to form its own state. Later, throughout the 1990s, even radical democratic critics of Milošević who rejected Serb nationalism acted on the presupposition that, among the ex-Yugoslav republics, it is only Serbia which shows democratic potential: after overthrowing Milošević, Serbia alone can turn into a thriving democratic state, while other ex-Yugoslav nations are too 'provincial' to sustain their own democratic state. Is this not the echo of Friedrich Engels's famous scathing remarks about how the small Balkan nations are politically reactionary since their very existence is a reaction, a survival of the past? Here we encounter a nice case of 'reflexive racism': of racism which assumes the very form of dismissing the Other as racist, intolerant, and so on.

No wonder, then, that in January 2002, at the congress of Spain's ruling centre-right People's Party, the Prime Minister, José Maria Aznar, praised Jürgen Habermas's concept of 'constitution-patriotism [*Verfassungspatriotismus*]', a patriotic attachment not to one's ethnic roots, but to the state's democratic constitution, which covers all its citizens equally. Aznar elevated this concept to the model for Spain, with its separatist troubles – mockingly, perhaps, he even proposed that the People's Party should declare Habermas Spain's official state philosopher. . . . Instead of dismissing this reference to the last great figure of the Frankfurt School as a ridiculous misunderstanding, we should, rather, identify the grain of truth in it: no wonder Basque 'separatists' reacted with mistrust, and even called Habermas a 'German nationalist' – they got the old 'Leninist' point that, in a state of ethnic tension, the apparently 'neutral' stance of indifference towards ethnic identity, of reducing all members of a state to mere abstract citizens, in fact favours the largest ethnic group.

In the Yugoslavia of the late 1980s, during the intense debate about its future, Serb intellectuals (precisely those who later opted for Milošević) also advocated the principle of abstract-neutral 'citizenship' – perhaps, then, there is more than a ridiculous idiosyncrasy in the fact – which is such an embarrassment to the Western followers of Habermas – that the majority of the Praxis group of Marxist philosophers from Serbia, who are close to the Frankfurt School tradition, ended up as Serb nationalists – some (like Mihajlo Marković) even as direct supporters and ideologists of Milošević. When, in the late 1980s, Zoran Djindjič, who is now the Serb Prime Minister, published a book in which he advocated a stronger unifying role for Serbia in Yugoslavia, he entitled it *Yugoslavia as an Unfinished Project* – a clear reference to Habermas's concept of modernity as an unfinished project. Confronted with these facts, followers of the Frankfurt School dismiss them as an unbelievable mystery, the onset of madness; let us imagine, however, that followers of Jacques Lacan were to take the same path – it is easy to imagine the vicious analyses of how such an engagement is a necessary outcome of Lacanian theory, along the lines of those who impute responsibility for Holocaust denial to 'deconstructionism'.

In 1980s Yugoslavia, then, did non-nationalist Communists really miss a golden opportunity to unite against Milošević on the democratic-socialist platform of saving Tito's legacy? This is arguably the most insidious pseudo-Leftist illusion. There actually was an attempt in 1989, at a meeting of the Politburo of the Yugoslav League of Communists dedicated to Tito's memory, to form a common front to defend Tito's legacy against the onslaught of Milošević's nationalism, and the spectacle was one of the saddest and most ridiculous ever seen. The 'democratic' Communists (the Croat Ivica Račan, who delivered the opening statement; the Slovene Milan Kučan, etc.) wanted to demonstrate what was obviously true, a kind of *vérité de la Palice*, namely, that the Serb nationalism endorsed by Milošević undermines the very foundations of Tito's Yugoslavia. The problem with this strategy was that it misfired miserably, because the 'democratic defenders of Tito' played themselves into a corner by adopting a ridiculously untenable and self-defeating position: in order to defend democratic potentials against the nationalist threat, they had to pretend to speak on behalf of the very ideology against which the democratic movement in Yugoslavia defined itself. In this way, they made it very easy for Milošević to get his message across: 'You are still possessed by the ghosts of an ideology which has lost its power, while I am the first politican who has fully assumed the consequences of the fact – which you disavow – that *Tito is dead!*'

So it was the very superficial fidelity to Tito's legacy which immobilized the majority in the Yugoslav League of the Communists, leaving the political initiative to Milošević: the truth of the sad spectacle of the late 1980s was that Milošević was making the rules and determining the political dynamics; he was acting, while other factions in the League of the Communists were merely reacting. The only way to counter Milošević effectively would have been, rather than clinging to old ghosts, to risk taking a step further than he did: openly to submit Tito's legacy itself to radical criticism. Or, to put it in more pathetic terms: it was not only Milošević who betrayed Tito's legacy; on a deeper level, the very anti-Milošević defenders of Titoism, representatives of local nomenklaturas worried about their privileges, were already clinging only to the corpse of ritualized Titoism – there was something justifiable in the way Milošević's populist movement overturned local nomenklaturas in Vojvodina and Montenegro (so-called 'yoghurt revolutions'). The only true defender of what was really worth saving in Tito's legacy was the Sarajevo government of independent Bosnia in the early 1990s.

So when Milošević in The Hague accuses the West of double standards, reminding Western leaders how less than a decade ago, when they already knew what they are accusing him of now, they hailed him as a peacemaker; when he threatens to bring *them* into the witness box, he is completely right. This is the true story of Milošević: not why he was singled out as the chief culprit, but why he was treated for so long as an acceptable partner – this story involves especially some West European powers like France and the UK, with their obvious pro-Serb bias. Again, Milošević is right: Western powers are also on trial in The Hague (albeit not in the sense intended by Milošević, of course). This was also the hypocritical aspect of the public outcry in the West at the beginning of March 2002 about the rigged elections in Zimbabwe: in abstract terms they were right; however, how was it possible for the problem of Zimbabwe to eclipse that of other African states where the human suffering caused by political dictatorship is incomparably greater – or, as a teacher from Kongo recently put it: 'Our misfortune is that we have gold, diamonds and precious wood, but, unfortunately, no white farmers.' That is to say: where was the West when, soon after independence, Mugabe ordered his infamous Fifth Brigade to murder over 20,000 opponents of his regime? The answer: it was too busy celebrating the wisdom of his concilia-tory politics towards white farmers to notice such details. . . .
The best way to illustrate the falsity of the American 'war against terrorism' is thus simply to *universalize* it: following America, other countries claimed the same right for

themselves – Israel (against the Palestinians), India (against Pakistan). What can we say to India, which now, after Pakistani-supported terrorists attacked its Parliament, claims the same right to military intervention in Pakistan? And what about all the past claims of governments against the United States government, which refused to extradite people who undoubtedly fitted the definition of 'terrorists' on which the USA is now relying?

Nevertheless, there is something exceptional about the Israeli–Palestinian conflict: it is clear that we are dealing with the *symptomal knot* of the Middle Eastern crisis, its Real which returns again and again to haunt all the participants. How often has it happened that a peace agreement seemed to be within reach, merely a matter of finding a proper formulation for some minor statements – then everything fell apart again, displaying the frailty of the symbolic compromise. The term 'symptomal knot' can be used quite literally here: is it not true that, in the Israeli–Palestinian conflict, the normal roles are somehow reversed, as in a knot? Israel – officially representing Western liberal modernity – legitimizes itself in terms of its ethnic-religious identity; while the Palestinians – decried as premodern 'fundamentalists' – legitimize their demands in terms of secular citizenship. If we argue that 'you can't really trust the Palestinians: given the chance, they would definitely slaughter and throw out the Israelis', we miss the point. Of course we should have no illusions about the Palestinians; the dream of a unified secular state in which Israelis and Palestinians would live happily side by side is, for the time being, just that, a dream – that is not the point. The point is simply that the IDF reservists' refusal revealed an aspect of the situation which totally undermines the simple opposition of civilized liberal Israelis fighting Islamic fanatics: the aspect, precisely, of reducing a whole nation to the status of *Homo sacer*, submitting them to a network of written and unwritten regulations which deprive them of their autonomy as members of a political community.

Let us, yet again, conduct a simple mental experiment: let us imagine the status quo in Israel and on the West Bank without any direct violence – what do we get? Not a normal peaceful state, but a group of people (Palestinians) subjected to systematic administrative hassle and deprivation (in terms of economic opportunities, the right to a water supply, permits to build houses, freedom of movement, etc.). When Benjamin Netanyahu made a speech to the American Congress as Prime Minister of Israel less than a decade ago, he emphatically rejected any division of Jerusalem, drawing a strange – if not downright obscene – parallel between Jerusalem and Berlin; in his impassioned plea, he asked why young Israeli couples should not have the same right as couples in big cities everywhere in the world: the right to move around and buy an apartment wherever they want to, in safety (invoking the same right, Ariel Sharon triggered unrest when he bought an apartment in the very heart of Arab Jerusalem, and visited it under heavy police protection). Of course, the obvious question arises here: would it be any less normal for a Palestinian to be able to buy an apartment anywhere he wants to in an undivided Jerusalem? This 'background noise', this underlying global imbalance, belies a simple consideration of 'who started it, and who did which violent act'.

How, then, are the two conflicts related – the 'war on terrorism' against al-Qaeda and the Israeli–Palestinian conflict? The key fact is the rather mysterious shift which occurred in spring 2002: all of a sudden, Afghanistan (and, up to a point, even the memory of the WTC attacks) was relegated to the background, and the focus shifted to the Israeli–Palestinian imbroglio. Two 'essentialist reductions' impose themselves: for the US and Israeli hawks, the 'war on terrorism' is the fundamental reference, and Israel's fight against the PLO is simply a subchapter in this struggle; Arafat is a terrorist like Bin Laden ('When the WTC towers and the Pentagon were hit by suicide bombers, the USA attacked Afghanistan, which was harbouring the attackers; when our cities are hit by suicide bombers, we have the same right to attack the Palestinian territories which harbour them!'); for the Arabs, the Israeli–Palestinian conflict is the fundamental reference, and the September 11 events are ultimately rooted in the injustice perpetrated by Israel and the USA against the Palestinians. This double 'essentialist reduction' should be linked to a double *je sais bien, mais quand même*: on the one hand, as a reaction to the wave of suicide bombings, many 'liberal' Israelis have adopted the stance of 'I don't support Sharon, but none the less . . . [in the present situation, we have to do something; Israel has the right to defend itself]'; on the other hand, many pro-Palestinian Western intellectuals have adopted the stance of 'I don't support the indiscriminate killing of Israeli civilians, but none the less . . . [the suicide bombings should be understood as desperate acts of the powerless against the Israeli military machine].'

When the problem is stated in these terms, then of course there is no way out; we are caught in an eternal self-perpetuating vicious cycle. The 'liberal' Israelis are right; we have to do something – but what? The conflict cannot be solved in its own terms: the only way to break out of the vicious cycle is through an act which would change the very co-ordinates of the conflict. Consequently, the problem with Ariel Sharon is not that he is overreacting, but that he is not doing enough, that he is not addressing the real problem – far from being a ruthless military executioner, Sharon is the model of a leader pursuing a confused politics of disorientated oscillation. The excessive Israeli military activity is ultimately an expression of impotence, an impotent *passage à l'acte* which, contrary to all appearances, does not have a clear goal: the obvious confusion about the true goals of Israeli military operations, the way they misfire again and again, and generate the opposite result of the intended one (pacification engenders more violence), is structural.

Perhaps the first move towards a solution is therefore to recognize this radical stalemate: by definition, neither side can win – the Israelis cannot occupy the entire Arab territory (Jordan, Syria, Lebanon, Egypt . . .), since the more land it occupies, the more it becomes vulnerable; the Arabs cannot destroy Israel militarily (not only because of its superiority in conventional arms, but also because Israel is a nuclear power: the old Cold War logic of MAD – Mutually Assured Destruction – is back in force here). Furthermore – for the moment, at least – a peaceful mixed Israeli–Palestinian society is unthinkable: in short, the Arabs will have to accept not only the existence of the State of Israel, but the existence of the *Jewish* State of Israel in their very midst, as a kind of ex-timate intruder. And, in all probability, this perspective also opens up the way for the only realistic solution to the deadlock: 'Kosovization', that is, the direct temporary presence in the occupied West Bank and Gaza territories of international (and – why not? – *NATO*) forces, which would simultaneously prevent Palestinian 'terror' and Israeli 'state terror', thus guaranteeing the conditions for both Palestinian statehood and Israeli peace.

In Palestine today, there are two opposing narratives with absolutely no common horizon, no 'synthesis' in a wider meta-narrative; thus the solution cannot be found in any all-encompassing narrative. This also means that when we consider this conflict we should stick to cold, ruthless standards, suspending the urge to try to 'understand' the situation: we should unconditionally resist the temptation to 'understand' Arab anti-Semitism (where we really encounter it) as a 'natural' reaction to the sad plight of the Palestinians; or to 'understand' the Israeli measures as a 'natural' reaction against the background of the memory of the Holocaust. There should be no 'understanding' for the fact that, in many – if not most – Arab countries, Hitler is still considered a hero; the fact that in primary-school textbooks all the traditional anti-Semitic myths – from the notorious forged Protocols of the Elders of Zion to claims that the Jews use the blood of Christian (or Arab) children for sacrificial purposes – are perpetrated. To claim that this anti-Semitism articulates resistance against capitalism in a displaced mode does not in any way justify it (the same goes for Nazi anti-Semitism: it, too, drew its energy from anticapitalist resistance): here displacement is not a secondary operation, but the fundamental gesture of ideological mystification. What this claim *does* involve is the idea that, in the long term, the only way to fight anti-Semitism is not to preach liberal tolerance, and so on, but to express the underlying anticapitalist motive in a direct, non-displaced way.

The key point is thus precisely not to interpret or judge single acts 'together', not to locate them in a 'wider context', but to excise them from their historical setting: the present actions of the Israeli Defence Forces on the West Bank should not be judged 'against the background of the Holocaust'; the fact that many Arabs celebrate Hitler, or that synagogues are desecrated in France and elsewhere in Europe, should not be judged as an 'inappropriate but understandable reaction to what the Israelis are doing in the West Bank'. This, however, does not in any way imply that we should not be extremely sensitive to the way concrete acts proposed today, even when they present themselves as 'progressive', may mobilize reactionary topics. In April 2002, in reaction to the Israeli military intervention in the Palestinian West Bank territory, a large group of Western European academics proposed a boycott of Israeli academic institutions (no invitations, no university exchanges, etc.); this proposal should be rejected, since the signifier 'Boycott the Jews!' carries a certain weight in Europe – there is no way we can eradicate, in a pseudo-Leninist way, the echo of the Nazi boycott of the Jews, claiming that, today, we are dealing with a 'different concrete historical situation'.

The Israeli–Palestinian conflict is, in the most radical sense of the term, a *false* conflict, a lure, an ideological displacement of the 'true' antagonism. Yes, the Arab 'fundamentalists' are 'Islamo-fascists' – in a repetition of the paradigmatic Fascist gesture, they want 'capitalism without capitalism' (without its excess of social disintegration, without its dynamics in which 'everything solid melts into air'). Yes, the Israelis stand for the principle of Western liberal tolerance, while, in their singularity, they embody the exception to this principle (advocating a state based on ethnic-religious identity – and this in a country with the highest percentage of atheists in the world). The Israeli reference to Western liberal tolerance, however, is the form of appearance of the neocolonialist terror of Capital; the call for 'unfreedom' (reactionary 'fundamentalism') is the form of appearance of the resistance to this terror.

When any public protest against Israeli Defence Forces activities in the West Bank is flatly denounced as an expression of anti-Semitism, and – implicitly, at least – put in the same category as defence of the Holocaust – that is to say, when the shadow of the Holocaust is permanently evoked in order to neutralize any criticism of Israeli military and political operations – it is not enough to insist on the difference between anti-Semitism and the critique of particular measures taken by the State of Israel; we should go a step further and claim that it is the State of Israel which, in this case, is desecrating the memory of the Holocaust victims: ruthlessly manipulating them, instrumentalizing them into a means of legitimizing current political measures. This means that we should reject out of

hand the very notion of any logical or political link between the
Holocaust and present Israeli–Palestinian tensions: they are two
completely different phenomena – one is part of the European
history of Rightist resistance to the dynamics of modernization;
the other is one of the last chapters in the history of colonization. On the other hand, the difficult task for the Palestinians is
to accept that their true enemies are not the Jews but Arab
regimes which manipulate their plight in order, precisely, to
prevent this shift – that is, the political radicalization in their
own states.

In the 'Special Davos Edition' of *Newsweek* (December
2001/February 2002), articles by two famous authors with
opposing views are published side by side: Samuel P.
Huntington's 'The Age of Muslim Wars' and Francis Fukuyama's
'The Real Enemy'. How, then, do they fit together – Francis
Fukuyama, with his pseudo-Hegelian idea of the 'end of history' (the final Formula for the best possible social order was
found with capitalist liberal democracy; there is now no room
for further conceptual progress, simply empirical obstacles to be
overcome); and Samuel P. Huntington, with his idea that the
'clash of civilizations' will be the main political struggle in the
twenty-first century? They both agree that militant fundamentalist Islam is the main threat today – so perhaps their views are
not really opposed, and we find the truth when we read them
together: *the 'clash of civilizations'* is *'the end of history'*. Pseudo-nat-
uralized ethnico-religious conflicts are the form of struggle
which fits global capitalism: in our age of 'post-politics', when
politics proper is progressively replaced by expert social administration, the only remaining legitimate source of conflicts is
cultural (ethnic, religious) tension. Today's rise of 'irrational'
violence should therefore be conceived as strictly correlative to
the depoliticization of our societies, that is, to the disappearance
of the proper political dimension, its translation into different

levels of 'administration' of social affairs: violence is accounted for in terms of social interests, and so on, and the unaccountable remainder cannot but appear to be 'irrational' . . . The properly Hegelian dialectical reversal is crucial here: what looks at first like the multitude of 'remainders of the past' which should be gradually overcome with the growth of a tolerant multicultural-ist liberal order is all of a sudden, in a flash of insight, perceived as this liberal order's very mode of existence – in short, teleo-logical temporal succession is unmasked as structural contemporaneity. (In exactly the same way, what, in the realm of 'really existing socialism', looked like petty-bourgeois 'remain-ders of the past', that eternal excuse for all the failures of socialist regimes, was the inherent product of the regime itself.)

So when Fukuyama talks about 'Islamo-Fascism', we should agree with him – on condition that we use the term 'Fascism' in a very precise way: as the name for the impossible attempt to have 'capitalism without capitalism', without the excesses of individualism, social disintegration, relativization of values, and so on. This means that the choice for the Muslims is not only either Islamo-Fascist fundamentalism or the painful process of 'Islamic Protestantism' which would make Islam compatible with modernization. There is a third option, which has already been tried: Islamic socialism. The proper politically correct atti-tude is to emphasize, with symptomatic insistence, how the terrorist attacks have nothing to do with the real Islam, that great and sublime religion – would it not be more appropriate to recognize Islam's resistance to modernization? And, rather than bemoaning the fact that Islam, of all the great religions, is the most resistant to modernization, we should, rather, conceive of this resistance as an open chance, as 'undecidable': this resist-ance does not necessarily lead to 'Islamo-Fascism', it could also be articulated into a Socialist project. Precisely because Islam harbours the 'worst' potentials of the Fascist answer to our present predicament, it could also turn out to be the site for the 'best'.

There is, then, an 'Arab question', in almost the same way as there was a 'Jewish question': is not the Arab–Jewish tension the ultimate proof of the continuing 'class struggle' in a displaced, mystified, 'post-political' form of the conflict between Jewish 'cosmopolitanism' and the Muslim rejection of modernity? In other words, what if the recurrence of anti-Semitism in today's globalized world provides the ultimate truth of the old Marxist insight that the only true 'solution' to this 'question' is Socialism?

CONCLUSION: THE SMELL
OF LOVE

In spring 2002, in the USA, one often met people proudly wearing a badge with the US and Israeli flags and the inscription 'United We Stand'. This new role for the Jews within the present global ideologico-political constellation – their privileged link to US-dominated global capitalism – is pregnant with horrifying dangers, opening up the way to outbursts of violent anti-Semitism: the fact that, due to a series of contingent strategic political decisions and conditions, Israel was elevated into the privileged partner of the USA may prove to be a source of new bloodshed. Consequently, the main task of all who really care for the Jewish people today is to work diligently towards severing this 'natural' link between the USA and the State of Israel. As we have seen, in the first round of the French presidential elections on April 21 2002, Jean-Marie le Pen, whose anti-Semitism is a constant factor (merely recall his remark that the Holocaust was a minor detail of European history), made it into the second round, emerging as the only alternative to Jacques Chirac – that is, beating Lionel Jospin, so that *the line of division is no longer between Right and Left, but between the global field of 'moderate' post-politics and extreme Rightist repoliticization*. Is not this shocking outcome an ominous sign of the price we are going to pay for the Pyrrhic victory of post-politics? That is to say: what we should always bear in mind is that Le Pen stands for the only serious political force in France which, in clear contrast to the suffocating lethargy of hegemonic post-politics, *persists in a stance of radical politicization*, of (perverted, but none the less 'live') political passion proper. To put it in Paulinen terms, the tragedy is that Le Pen, in his very repulsive provocation, stands for Life against post-political Death as the way of life of the Last Men.

The worst thing to do apropos of the events of September 11 is to elevate them to a point of Absolute Evil, a vacuum which cannot be explained and/or dialecticized. To put them in the same league as the Shoah is a blasphemy: the Shoah was committed in a methodical way by a vast network of state *apparatchiks* and their minions who, in contrast to those who attacked the WTC towers, lacked the suicidal acceptance of their own death – as Hannah Arendt made clear, they were anonymous bureaucrats doing their job, and an enormous gap separated what they did from their individual self-experience. This 'banality of Evil' is missing in the case of the terrorist attacks: the perpetrators fully assumed the horror of their acts; this horror is part of the fatal attraction which draws them towards committing them. Or, to put it slightly differently: the Nazis did their job of 'solving the Jewish question' as an obscene secret hidden from the public gaze, while the terrorists openly displayed the spectacle of their act. The second difference is that the Shoah was part of *European* history; it was an event which is not directly linked with the relationship between Muslims and Jews: remember Sarajevo, which had by far the largest Jewish community in ex-Yugoslavia, and, moreover, was the most cosmopolitan Yugoslav city, the thriving centre of cinema and rock music – why? Precisely because it was the Muslim-dominated city, where the Jewish and Christian presence was tolerated, in contrast to the Christian-dominated large cities from which Jews and Muslims were purged long ago.

Why should the World Trade Center catastrophe be in any way privileged over, say, the mass slaughter of Hutus by Tutsis in Rwanda in 1994? Or the mass bombing and gas-poisoning of Kurds in the north of Iraq in the early 1990s? Or the Indonesian forces' mass killings in East Timor? Or . . . the list of countries where the mass suffering was and is incomparably greater than the suffering in New York, but which do not have the luck to be elevated by the media into the sublime victim of Absolute Evil, is long, and that is the point: if we insist on the use of this term, these are all 'Absolute Evils'. So should we extend the prohibition to explain, and claim that none of these evils could or should be 'dialecticized'? And are we not obliged to go even a step further: what about horrible 'individual' crimes, from those of the sadistic mass murderer Jeffrey Dahmer to that of Andrea Yates, who drowned her five children in cold blood? Is there not something real/impossible/inexplicable about *all* of these acts? Is it not that – as Schelling put it more than two hundred years ago – in each of them we confront the ultimate abyss of free will, the imponderable fact of 'I did it because I did it!' which resists any explanation in terms of psychological, social, ideological, etc., causes?

In short, is it not that today, in our resigned postideological era which admits no positive Absolutes, the only legitimate candidate for the Absolute are radically evil acts? This negative-theological status of the Holocaust finds its supreme expression in Giorgio Agamben's *Remnants of Auschwitz*, in which he provides a kind of ontological proof of Auschwitz against revisionists who deny the Holocaust. He directly concludes the existence of the Holocaust from its 'concept' (notions like the living-dead 'Muslims' are so 'intense' that they could not have emerged without the fact of the Holocaust) – what better proof is there that, in some of today's cultural studies, the Holocaust is in fact elevated to the dignity of the Thing, perceived as the negative Absolute? And it tells us a lot about today's constellation that the only Absolute is that of sublime/irrepresentable Evil. Agamben refers to the four modal categories (possibility, impossibility, contingency, necessity), articulating them along the axis of subjectification–desubjectification: possibility (to be able to be) and contingency (to be able not to be) are the operators of subjectification; while impossibility (not to be able to be) and necessity (not to be able not to be) are the operators of desubjectification – and what happens in Auschwitz is the point at which the two sides of the axis fall together:

> Auschwitz represents the historical point at which these processes collapse, the devastating experience in which the impossible is forced into the real. Auschwitz is the existence of the impossible, the most radical negation of contingency; it is, therefore, absolute necessity. The *Muselmann* [the 'living dead' of the camp] produced by Auschwitz is the catastrophe of the subject that then follows, the subject's effacement as the place of contingency and its maintenance as existence of the impossible.[52]

Thus Auschwitz designates the catastrophe of a kind of ontological short circuit: subjectivity (the opening of the space of contingency in which possibility counts more than actuality) collapses into the objectivity in which it is impossible for things not to follow 'blind' necessity. In order to grasp this point, we should consider the two aspects of the term 'impossibility': first, impossibility as the simple obverse of necessity ('it couldn't have been

52 Giorgio Agamben, *Remnants of Auschwitz*, New York: Zone Books 1999, p. 148.

otherwise'); then, impossibility as the ultimate unthinkable limit of possibility itself ('something so horrible cannot really happen; nobody can be so evil') – in Auschwitz, the two aspects coincide. We can even put it in Kantian terms, as the short circuit between the noumenal and the phenomenal: in the figure of *Muselmann*, the living dead, the desubjectivized subject, the noumenal dimension (of the free subject) appears in empirical reality itself – *Muselmann* is the noumenal Thing directly appearing in phenomenal reality; as such, it is the witness of what one cannot bear witness to. And, in a further step, Agamben reads this unique figure of *Muselmann* as the irrefutable proof of the existence of Auschwitz:

> Let us, indeed, posit Auschwitz, that to which it is not possible to bear witness, and let us also posit the *Muselmann* as the absolute impossibility of bearing witness. If the witness bears witness for the *Muselmann*, if he succeeds in bringing to speech an impossibility of speech – if the *Muselmann* is thus constituted as the whole witness – then the denial of Auschwitz is refuted in its very foundation. In the *Muselmann*, the impossibility of bearing witness is no longer a mere privation. Instead, it has become real; it exists as such. If the survivor bears witness not to the gas chambers or to Auschwitz but to the *Muselmann*, if he speaks only on the basis of an impossibility of speaking, then his testimony cannot be denied. Auschwitz – that to which it is not possible to bear witness – is absolutely and irrefutably proven.[53]

We cannot but admire the finesse of this theorization: far from hindering any proof that Auschwitz really existed, the very fact

---

53 Ibid., p. 164.

that it is impossible directly to bear witness to Auschwitz demonstrates its existence. There, in this reflexive twist, lies the fatal miscalculation of the well-known cynical Nazi argument quoted by Primo Levi and others: 'What we are doing to the Jews is so irrepresentable in its horror that even if someone survives the camps, he will not be believed by those who were not there – they will simply declare him a liar or mentally ill!' Agamben's counterargument is: true, it is not possible to bear witness to the ultimate horror of Auschwitz – but what if *this impossibility itself is embodied in a survivor*? If, then, there is a subjectivity like that of the *Muselmann*, a subjectivity brought to the extreme point of collapsing into objectivity, *such desubjectivized subjectivity could have emerged only in the conditions which are those of Auschwitz.* . . . None the less, this line of argument, inexorable as it is in its very simplicity, remains deeply ambiguous: it leaves unaccomplished the task of the concrete analysis of the historical singularity of the Holocaust. That is to say: it is possible to read it in two opposed ways – as the conceptual expression of a certain extreme position which should then be accounted for in the terms of a concrete historical analysis; or, in a kind of ideological short circuit, as an insight into the a priori structure of the Auschwitz phenomenon which displaces, renders superfluous – or, at least, secondary – such a concrete analysis of the singularity of Nazism as a political project and of why it generated the Holocaust. In this second reading, 'Auschwitz' becomes the name of something which, in a way, *had* to happen, whose 'essential possibility' was inscribed into the very matrix of the Western political process – sooner or later, the two sides of the axis *had* to collapse.

Have the events of September 11, then, something to do with the obscure God who demands human sacrifices? Yes – and, precisely for that reason, they are not on the same level as the Nazi annihilation of the Jews. Here, one should follow

Agamben[54] and reject Lacan's famous reading of the Holocaust (the Nazi extermination of the Jews) as, precisely, the holocaust in the old Jewish meaning of the term, the sacrifice to the obscure gods, destined to satisfy their terrible demand for *jouissance*:[55] the annihilated Jews belong, rather, to the species of what the Ancient Romans called *Homo sacer* – those who, although they were human, were excluded from the human community, which is why one can kill them with impunity – *and, for that very reason, one cannot sacrifice them (because they are not a worthy sacrificial offering).*[56]

The spectacular explosion of the WTC towers was not simply a symbolic act (in the sense of an act whose aim is to 'deliver a message'): it was primarily an explosion of lethal *jouissance*, a perverse act of making oneself an instrument of the big Other's *jouissance*. Yes, the culture of the attackers is a morbid culture of death, the attitude which finds the climactic fulfilment of one's own life in violent death. The problem is not what the 'insane fanatics' are doing, but what the 'rational strategists' behind them are doing. There is much more ethical insanity in a military strategist planning and executing large-scale bombing operations than in an individual blowing himself

---

54 See Agamben, *Homo Sacer.*

55 Jacques Lacan, *The Four Fundamental Concepts of Pycho-Analysis*, New York: Norton 1979, p. 253.

56 Why, then, did the term 'holocaust', although it was a misnomer, gain such currency among Jews and Gentiles alike? It softens the traumatic core of the annihilation of the Jews by conceiving of it as a (perverse, but none the less ultimately) meaningful sacrificial operation: better to be the precious sacrificed object than a worthless *Homo sacer* whose death counts for nothing. . . . In 2000, a big scandal was caused in Israel by the claim of an orthodox rabbi leader that the six million Jews killed by the Nazis were not innocent: their killing was a justified punishment; they must have been guilty of betraying God. . . . The lesson of this bizarre anecdote is, again, our extreme difficulty in accepting the meaninglessness of utter catastrophe.

up in the process of attacking the enemy. Yes, the ultimate aim
of the attacks was not some hidden or obvious ideological
agenda, but – precisely in the Hegelian sense of the term – to
(re)introduce the dimension of absolute negativity into our daily
lives: to shatter the insulated daily course of the lives of us, true
Nietzschean Last Men. Long ago, Novalis made the perspicuous
observation that what an evil man hates is not the good – he
hates evil excessively (the world which he considers evil), and
therefore tries to hurt and destroy it as much as possible – *this*
is what is wrong with the 'terrorists'. Sacrilegious as it may
appear, the WTC attacks do share something with Antigone's
act: they both undermine the 'servicing of goods', the reign of
the pleasure-reality principle. The 'dialectical' thing to do here,
however, is not to include these acts in some wider narrative of
the Progress of Reason or Humanity, which somehow, if it does
not redeem them, at least makes them part of an all-encompassing wider consistent narrative, 'sublates' them in a 'higher'
stage of development (the naive notion of Hegelianism), but to
make us question our own innocence, to render thematic our
own (fantasmatic libidinal) investment and engagement in them.

So, rather than remain stuck in debilitating awe in front of
Absolute Evil, the awe which stops us from thinking about what
is going on, we should remember that there are two fundamental ways of reacting to such traumatic events, which cause
unbearable anxiety: the way of the superego and the way of the
act. The way of the superego is precisely that of the sacrifice to
the obscure gods of which Lacan speaks: the reassertion of the
barbaric violence of the savage obscene law in order to fill in the
gap of the failing symbolic law. And the act? One of the heroes
of the Shoah for me is a famous Jewish ballerina who, as a gesture of special humiliation, was asked by the camp officers to
dance for them. Instead of refusing, she did it, and while she
held their attention, she quickly grabbed the machine-gun from

one of the distracted guards and, before being shot down her-self, succeeded in killing more than a dozen officers. . . . Was not her act comparable to that of the passengers on the flight which crashed in Pennsylvania who, knowing that they would die, forced their way into the cockpit and crashed the plane, saving hundreds of others' lives?

According to the Ancient Greek myth, Europa was a Phoenician princess abducted and then raped by Zeus in the guise of a bull – no wonder her name means 'the dismal one'. Is this not a true picture of Europe? Did not Europe (as an ideo-logical notion) arise as the outcome of two such abductions of an Eastern pearl by barbarians from the West: first, the Romans abducted and vulgarized Greek thought; then, in the early Middle Ages, the barbarian West abducted and vulgarized Christianity? And is not something similar going on today for the third time? Is not the 'war on terrorism' the abominable con-clusion, the 'dotting of the i', of a long, gradual process of American ideological, political and economic colonization of Europe? Was not Europe again kidnapped by the West – by American civilization, which is now setting global standards and, *de facto*, treating Europe as its province?

After the World Trade Center attacks, the big story in the media was the rise of anti-American *Schadenfreude* and the lack of simple human sympathy with American suffering among the European intelligentsia. The true story, however, is exactly the opposite one: the total lack of an autonomous European politi-cal initiative. In the aftermath of September 11, Europe – the key states of the European Union – took the path of 'uncondi-tional compromise', giving in to US pressure. The war in Afghanistan, the plans for an attack on Iraq, the new explosion of violence in Palestine: each time, there were muffled voices of discontent in Europe which raised particular points, and calls for a more balanced approach; however, there was no formal resistance, no imposition of a different global perception of the crisis. No official European institution risked a friendly but clear distantiation from the American position. No wonder, then, that these voices of protest died away – they were literally *of no consequence*, mere empty gestures whose function was to enable us, Europeans, to say to ourselves: 'You see, we did protest, we did our duty!', while silently endorsing the *fait accompli* of American politics.

This fiasco reached its high point with the Israeli invasion of the West Bank, where the situation itself calls for a new political initiative, which is the only thing that can break the present deadlock. The most frustrating aspect of this crisis is that nothing can be done, although everyone is aware of how, basically, the solution should look: two states, Israel and Palestine; the evacuation of the Jewish West Bank settlements in exchange for full recognition of Israel, and its safety. (Everyone, that is, except Israeli hardliners and their US supporters: in a radio talk at the beginning of May 2002, Dick Arney, the minority leader of the US Senate, advocated a thorough 'ethnic cleansing' of the West Bank – the Palestinians should simply be made to leave. . . . Is this not also the true hidden agenda of the recent Israeli military action?) Europe is in an ideal position to start such an initiative – on condition that it summons up the strength to distance itself clearly from the American hegemony. Now that the Cold War is over, there are no serious external obstacles to such a gesture: Europe should simply take courage and *do it*.

As a result, the real politico-ideological catastrophe of September 11 was that of Europe: the result of September 11 is an unprecedented strengthening of American hegemony, in all its aspects. Europe succumbed to a kind of ideologico-political blackmail by the USA: 'What is now at stake are no longer different economical or political choices, but our very survival – in the war on terrorism, you are either with us or against us.' And it is here, at this point where the reference to mere survival enters the scene as the ultimate legitimization, that we are dealing with political ideology at its purest. In the name of the 'war on terrorism', a certain positive vision of global political relations is silently imposed on us Europeans. And if the emancipatory legacy of Europe is to survive, we should take the September 11 fiasco as the last warning that time is running out, that Europe should move quickly to assert itself *as an autonomous ideological, political and economic force, with its own priorities*. It is a unified Europe, not Third World resistance to American imperialism, that is the only feasible counterpoint to the USA and China as the two global superpowers. The Left should unashamedly appropriate the slogan of a unified Europe as a counterweight to Americanized globalism.

And the New Yorkers themselves? For months after September 11 2001, it was possible to smell in downtown Manhattan up to 20th Street the scent of the burning WTC towers – people became attached to this smell, it started to function as what Lacan would have called the 'sinthome' of New York, a condensed cipher of the subject's libidinal attachment to the city, so that when it disappears it will be missed. It is such details that bear witness to a true love of the city. This love only becomes problematic when it turns into the suspicion of why others do not fully share America's pain, as in the standard complaint addressed by many American liberals to the European Leftists – they did not show enough sincere compassion with the victims of September 11 attacks. Along the same lines, the American reproach to European criticism of its politics is that this is a case of envy and frustration at being reduced to the secondary role, of the European inability to accept one's limitation and (relative) decline; however, is it not the opposite which holds even more? Is not the surprise at why are they not loved for what they are doing to the world the most fundamental

American reaction (at least) since the Vietnam war? We just try to be good, to help others, to bring peace and prosperity, and look what we get in return. . . . The fundamental insight of movies like John Ford's Searchers and Michael Scorsese's Taxi Driver is still more than relevant.

These complaints are sustained by the more fundamental unspoken reproach that Europeans do not really share the American Dream – the reproach is in a way fully justified: the Third World cannot generate a strong enough resistance to the ideology of the American Dream; in the present constellation, it is only Europe which can do it. The true opposition today is not the one between the First World and the Third World, but the one between the whole of the First and Third World (the American global Empire and its colonies) and the remaining Second World (Europe). Apropos Freud, Adorno claimed that what we are getting in contemporary 'administered world' and its 'repressive desublimation' is no longer the old logic of repression of the Id and its drives, but a perverse direct pact between the Superego (social authority) and the Id (illicit aggressive drives) at the expense of the Ego. Is not something structurally similar going on today at the political level, the weird pact between the postmodern global capitalism and the premodern societies at the expense of modernity proper? It is easy for the American multiculturalist global Empire to integrate premodern local traditions – the foreign body which it effectively cannot assimilate is the European modernity. Jihad and McWorld are the two sides of the same coin, Jihad is already McJihad.

The key news from China in 2002 was the emergence of large-scale workers movement, protesting against the work conditions which are the price for China rapidly becoming the world's foremost manufacturing place, and the brutal way the authorities cracked down on it – a new proof, if one is still needed, that China is today the ideal capitalist state: freedom for the capital, with the state doing the 'dirty job' of controlling the workers. China as the emerging superpower of the twenty-first century thus seems to embody a new kind of ruthless capitalism: disregard for ecological consequences, disregard for workers' rights, everything subordinated to the ruthless drive to develop and become the new superpower. The big question is: what will the Chinese do with regard to the biogenetic revolution? Is it not a safe wager that they will throw themselves into unconstrained genetic manipulations of plants, animals and humans, bypassing all our 'Western' moral prejudices and limitations? And, with the further expansion of the biogenetic technology, which is relatively inexpensive (Cuba is already highly developed in this area), will not the same hold for many a Third World country? (Although, of course, it is also true that – till now, at least – China is definitely the superpower with by far the lowest level of imperialist interventions, of trying to expand its influence and control its neighbours.)

The tension between America and Europe is discernible even within (what remains of) the political Left: the 'americanization' is here under the guise of the notion that the Left should fully endorse the dynamics of globalization, the deterritorializing multitude of late capitalism. . . . Michael Hardt and Negri discern two ways to oppose the global capitalist Empire: either the 'protectionist' advocacy of the return to the strong Nation-State, or the deployment of the even more flexible forms of multitude. Along these lines, in his analysis of the Porto Alegre anti-globalist meeting, Hardt emphasizes the new logic of the political space there: it was no longer the old 'us versus them' binary logic with the Leninist call for a firm singular party line, but the coexistence of a multitude of political agencies and positions which shared the same platform, despite being incompatible as to their ideological and programmatic accents (from 'conservative' farmers and ecologists worried about the fate of their local tradition and patrimony, to human rights groups and agents standing for the

interests of immigrants, advocating global mobility). It is effectively today's opposition to global capital which seems to provide
a kind of negative mirror-image to Deleuze's claim about the
inherently antagonistic claim of the capitalist dynamics (a strong
machine of deterritorialization which generates new modes of
reterritorialization): today's resistance to capitalism reproduces
the same antagonism; calls for the defence of particular (cultural,
ethnic) identities being threatened by the global dynamics coexist with the demands for more global mobility (against the new
barriers imposed by capitalism, which concern above all the free
movement of individuals). Is it then true that these tendencies
(these *lignes de fuite*, as Deleuze would have put it) can coexist in
a non-antagonistic way, as parts of the same global network of
resistance? One is tempted to answer this claim by applying to it
Laclau's notion of the chain of equivalences: of course this logic
of multitude functions – because we are still dealing with *resistance*. However, what about when – if this really is the desire and
will of these movements – 'we take it over'? What would the
'multitude in power' look like? There was the same constellation
in the last years of the decaying Really-Existing Socialism: the
non-antagonistic coexistence, within the oppositional field, of a
multitude of ideologico-political tendencies, from liberal
human-rights groups to 'liberal' business-oriented groups, conservative religious groups and Leftist workers' demands. This
multitude functioned well as long as it was united in the opposition to 'them', the Party hegemony; once they found
themselves in power, the game was over. . . . Furthermore, is the
State today really withering away (with the advent of the much-
praised liberal 'deregulation')? Is, on the contrary, the 'war
on terror' not the strongest assertion yet of state authority? Are
we not witnessing now the unheard-of mobilization of all
(repressive and ideological) state apparatuses?

These state apparatuses play a crucial role in the obverse side of globalization. Recently, an ominous decision of the European Union passed almost unnoticed: the plan to establish an all-European border police force to secure the isolation of the Union territory and thus to prevent the influx of immigrants. *This* is the truth of globalization: the construction of *new* walls safeguarding prosperous Europe from the immigrant flood. One is tempted to resuscitate here the old Marxist 'humanist' opposition of 'relations between things' and 'relations between persons': in the much celebrated free circulation opened up by global capitalism, it is 'things' (commodities) which freely circulate, while the circulation of 'persons' is more and more controlled. This new racism of the developed world is in a way much more brutal than the previous ones: its implicit legitimization is neither naturalist (the 'natural' superiority of the developed West) nor any longer culturalist (we in the West also want to preserve our cultural identity), but unabashed economic egotism – the fundamental divide is the one between those included into the sphere of (relative) economic prosperity and those excluded from it. What lies beneath these protective measures is the simple awareness that the present model of late capitalist prosperity *cannot be universalized* – the awareness formulated with a brutal candour more than half a century ago by George Kennan:

> We [the USA] have 50 per cent of the world's wealth but only 6.3 per cent of its population. In this situation, our real job in the coming period . . . is to maintain this position of disparity. To do so, we have to dispense with all sentimentality . . . we should cease thinking about human rights, the raising of living standards and democratisation.[57]

57 George Kennan in 1948, quoted in John Pilger, *The New Rulers Of the World*, London and New York: Verso 2002, p. 98.

And the sad thing is that, concerning this fundamental awareness, there is a silent pact between the Capital and (whatever
remains of) the working classes – if anything, the working
classes are *more* sensitive to the protection of their relative privileges than the big corporations. This, then, is the *truth* of the
discourse of universal human rights: *the Wall separating those
covered by the umbrella of Human Rights and those excluded from its
protective cover*. Any reference to universal human rights as an
'unfinished project' to be gradually extended to all people is
here a vain ideological chimera – and, faced with this prospect,
do we, in the West, have any right to condemn the excluded
when they use any means, inclusive of terror, to fight their
exclusion?

This, then, is the test of how seriously we take the
Derridean–Levinasian topic of hospitality and openness towards
the Other: again, this topic means hospitality towards the immigrants (or Palestinians in Israel) *or it means nothing*. It may appear
that Israel is merely reacting to the Palestinian terrorist attacks;
however, what goes on *beneath* this cycle of actions and reactions
is not nothing, the status quo, but the continuing silent Israeli
expansion into the occupied territories – the colonization is pro-
gressing all the time, and even now, in the spring of 2002, after
the violent explosion when Israel claimed that its very existence
was threatened, it started to build 30 *new* West Bank settlements. Even under the Barak government, which allegedly
offered the Palestinians the largest possible concessions, the
building of new settlements continued faster than under the
previous Netanyahu government. This continuous expansion
(which clearly aims at creating an irreversible situation in which
the complete withdrawal of Israel from the West Bank will be
impossible) is the *basic* fact to which the Palestinian terror reacts,
the silent continuous murmur, that which happens, which goes
on when, for the big media, 'nothing is happening'. (And one

should not forget that terror – bombing in crowded civilian places – is an old anticolonial weapon, practised also by Algerians and others, inclusive of Jews themselves against the British occupation of Palestine in the late 1940s.)

No wonder, then, that, in a kind of echo to European Unity, in June 2002, Israel also started to raise the protective Wall against the West Bank Arab settlements. When terrorists are more and more described in the terms of a viral infection, as an attack of invisible bacteria, one should recall that the comparison of Jews to 'bacteria' attacking the sane social body is one of the classic topoi of anti-Semitism. Is then the invisible fundamentalist terrorist the last embodiment of the Wandering Jew? Are today's reports on the secret Muslim fundamentalist plans to destroy the West the new version of the infamous Protocols of the Zion? Does today's 'war on terror' signal the paradoxical point at which *the Zionist jews themselves joined the ranks of anti-Semitism*? Is this the ultimate price of the establishment of the Jewish *State*?

What underlies these ominous strategies is the fact that democracy (the established liberal-democratic parliamentary system) is no longer 'alive' in the Paulinian sense of the term: the tragic thing is that the only serious political force which is today 'alive' is the new populist Right. Insofar as we play the democratic game of leaving the place of power empty, of accepting the gap between this place and our occupying it (which is the very gap of castration), are we – democrats – all not 'fidel castros', faithful to castration? Apart from anaemic economic administration, the liberal-democratic centre's main function is to guarantee that nothing will really happen in politics: liberal democracy is the party of non-Event. The line of division is more and more 'Long live . . . Le Pen, Haider, Berlusconi!' versus 'Death to . . . the same!' – with the opposition life/death adequately distributed between the two poles. Or, to put it in

Nietzschean terms (as they were interpreted by Deleuze): today, the populist Right *acts*, sets the pace, determines the problematic of the political struggle, and the liberal centre is reduced to a 'reactive force': it ultimately limits itself to *reacting* to the populist Right's initiatives, either opposing them radically from an impotent Leftist posturing, or translating them into the acceptable liberal language ('while rejecting the populist hatred of the immigrants, we have to admit they are addressing issues which really worry people, so we should take care of the problem, introduce tougher immigration and anti-crime measures . . .').

The notion of the radical political Act as the way out of this democratic deadlock, of course, cannot but provoke the expected reaction from the liberals. The standard critique concerns the Act's allegedly 'absolute' character of a radical break, which renders impossible any clear distinction between a properly 'ethical' act and, say, a Nazi monstrosity: is it not that an Act is always embedded in a specific socio-symbolic context? The answer to this reproach is clear: of course – an Act is always a specific intervention within a socio-symbolic context; the *same* gesture can be an Act or a ridiculous empty posture, depending on this context (say, making a public ethical statement when it is too late changes a courageous intervention into an irrelevant gesture). In what, then, resides the misunderstanding? Why this critique? There is something else which disturbs the critics of the Lacanian notion of Act: true, an Act is always situated in a concrete context – this, however, does not mean that it is fully determined by its context. An Act always involves a radical risk, what Derrida, following Kierkegaard, called the *madness* of a decision: it is a step into the open, with no guarantee about the final outcome – why? Because an Act retroactively changes the very co-ordinates into which it intervenes. This lack of guarantee is what the critics cannot tolerate: they want an Act without risk — not without empirical risks, but without the much more radical 'transcendental risk' that the Act will not only simply fail, but radically misfire. In short, to paraphrase Robespierre, those who oppose the 'absolute Act' effectively oppose the Act *as such*, they want an Act without the Act. What they want is homologous to the 'democratic' opportunists who, as Lenin put it in the autumn of 1917, want a 'democratically legitimized' revolution, as if one should first organize a referendum, and only then, after obtaining a clear majority, seize power . . . It is here that one can see how an Act proper cannot be contained within the limits of democracy (conceived as a positive system of legitimizing power through free elections). The Act occurs in an emergency when one has to take the risk and act without any legitimization, engaging oneself into a kind of Pascalean wager that the Act itself will create the conditions of its retroactive 'democratic' legitimization. Say, when, in 1940, after the French defeat, de Gaulle called for the continuation of warfare against the Germans, his gesture was without 'democratic legitimization' (at that moment, a large majority of the French were unambiguously supporting Marshall Petain — Jacques Duclos, the leading French Communist, wrote that, if 'free elections' were to be held in France in the autumn of 1940, Petain would have got at least 90 per cent of the votes). However, in spite of this lack of 'democratic legitimization', the *truth* was on de Gaulle's side, and he effectively *was* speaking on behalf of France, of the French people 'as such'. This also enables us to answer the ultimate democratic reproach: the absolute (self-referential) act is deprived of any external control which would prevent terrifying excesses — anything can be legitimized in a self-referential way? The answer is clear: as (among others) the case of France in 1940 demonstrates, democracy itself cannot provide such a guarantee; *there is no guarantee* against the possibility of the excess – the risk *has* to be assumed, it is part of the very field of the political.

And, perhaps, the ultimate aim of the 'war on terror', of the imposition of what one cannot but call the 'democratic state of emergency', is to neutralize the conditions of such an Act. According to an old Marxist topos, the evocation of the external enemy serves to displace the focus from the true origin of tensions, the inherent antagonism of the system – recall the standard explanation of anti-Semitism as the displacement onto the figure of the Jew, this *external* intruder into our social body, of the cause of the antagonisms which threaten the harmony of this body. There is, however, also the opposite ideological operation, the false evocation of *internal* causes of failure. In 1940, when Petain became the French leader, he explained the French defeat as the result of a long process of degeneration of the French state caused by the liberal-Jewish influence; so, according to Petain, the French defeat was a blessing in disguise, a shattering and painful reminder of one's weaknesses and thus a chance to reconstitute French strength on a healthy base. Do we not find the same motif in many a conservative critic of today's permissive-consumerist Western societies? The ultimate threat does not come from out there, from the fundamentalist Other, but from within, from our own lassitude and moral weakness, loss of clear values and firm commitments, of the spirit of dedication and sacrifice. . . . No wonder that, in their first reaction, Jerry Falwell and Pat Robertson claimed that, on September 11, the USA got what it deserved. What, then, if exactly the same logic sustains the 'war on terror'? What if the true aim of this 'war' is *ourselves*, our own ideological mobilization against the threat of the Act? What if the 'terrorist attack', no matter how 'real' and terrifying, is ultimately a metaphoric substitute for this Act, for the shattering of our liberal-democratic consensus?